10-MINUTE IDEAS
FOR EARLY YEARS

Creative fun

OXFO
U

D1396009

Alison Coleman

■ **Quick activities for any time of the day**
■ **Links to Early Learning Goals** ■ **Time-saving photocopiables**

Credits

Author
Alison Coleman

Editor
Jane Bishop

Assistant Editor
Margaret Eaton

Series Designer
Anna Oliwa

Designer
Andrea Lewis

Cover Illustration
Craig Cameron/Art
Collection

Illustrations
Bethan Matthews

Text © 2005 Alison Coleman
© 2005 Scholastic Ltd

Designed using Adobe InDesign

Published by Scholastic Ltd
Villiers House
Clarendon Avenue
Leamington Spa
Warwickshire
CV32 5PR

www.scholastic.co.uk

Printed by Bell & Bain Ltd

1 2 3 4 5 6 7 8 9   5 6 7 8 9 0 1 2 3 4

British Library Cataloguing-in-Publication Data
A catalogue record for this book is available from the British Library.

ISBN 0-439-97160-8
ISBN 978-0439-97160-7

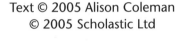

Contents

Contents

Introduction

Creative play is a cornerstone of skills development in young children. Social skills, physical co-ordination, numeracy, literacy and innovation can all be enhanced through structured and stimulating creative play ideas. The activities in this book are designed to help early years practitioners focus on specific areas of skills development, and to provide a means of assessing the various stages that each child has reached.

The activities are divided into six chapters, each representing an area of creative play. These include painting, drawing, construction, collages, paper crafts and modelling. The activities within each chapter encompass the six Areas of Learning, as set out in the *Curriculum Guidance for the Foundation Stage* (QCA). By arranging the contents in this way, practitioners can plan their play activity schedules to include a mix of creative mediums while focusing on one learning area, such as Mathematical development or Physical development. This flexibility ensures variety and a degree of repetition for the children – for example, in learning to form letters and to recognise number shapes through drawing and modelling activities.

Some of the activities will encourage young children to become more observant about their home and local environment, while others require co-operation between individual children and are aimed at fostering greater consideration for each other's feelings and opinions.

Creative play will help to stimulate a child's own imagination. Where possible, activities are designed for children to input their own choices and ideas. Any comments or suggestions they make for carrying out an activity in a different or better way, should be encouraged. The successful completion of a collage or model is a valuable boost to their self-confidence. Many of the ideas involve displaying finished craftwork in the most interesting or attractive way. Children should be encouraged to offer their opinions on what they think produces the best result.

While each activity is designed with a specific educational purpose, the most important thing is to make them fun to carry out.

Using the activities

The activities in the book are designed to be carried out in a relatively short space of time, with a minimum of preparation. Group sizes vary from two to ten children, and can therefore be used to encourage teamwork and the development of social skills, or independent work and the development of imaginative play and problem solving.

Some activities require illustrations to clarify the procedure, for which photocopiable pages are provided. Each activity includes a step-by-step guide to help ensure successful results, with additional guidance for helping younger children complete the activities and extension ideas for older children. At the end of each activity, a home link offers suggestions as to how parents and carers can help children transfer their developing skills into the home environment.

When setting up for creative play you may need to protect your work surfaces with newspaper or plastic covers, and provide the children with aprons.

Stepping Stones and Early Learning Goals

Each of the six chapters in the book covers the six Areas of Learning, and each activity is linked to a particular Stepping Stone and Early Learning Goal. This enables practitioners to ensure they have comprehensive coverage of all areas. At the end of each activity there are a number of further ideas, which give suggestions for ideas and activities related to the Stepping Stone or Early Learning Goal.

Assessing the activities

The extension ideas that accompany each activity serve as useful indicators of a child's ability to complete it independently. A child who is able to carry out the activity without any extra help or support can be said to have mastered the relevant Stepping Stone. Those who need extra help or encouragement have not quite achieved the Stepping Stone.

How to use this book

Because the activities can be completed in a fairly short space of time they can easily be incorporated into a daily or weekly schedule without a great deal of forward planning. However one or two of the activities, such as Autumn leaves on page 10 and Nature collage on page 45 have a seasonal element and need to be planned for accordingly. Many of the activities are flexible enough to be incorporated into the marking or celebration of religious festivals or special holidays, and again these need to be prepared a little further in advance.

Some of the activities for larger groups of children underpin the concepts of sharing, taking turns, and showing consideration for others, while activities designed for smaller groups allow practitioners to closely assess individual progress across a range of skills.

Painting

Use the ideas in this chapter to extend the children's skills across all areas of the curriculum. Encourage them to try out different types of paint with brushes, straws and other craft materials to achieve a range of exciting creations.

Pebble painting

What you need
An assortment of fairly large pebbles (some smooth and flat, others round and rougher edged); large container; poster paints; brushes; clear lacquer; aprons; newspaper.

Preparation
Protect work surfaces and floors with newspaper and ask the children to put on their aprons. Place the pebbles in a large container so that the children can see all of them easily.

What to do
Ask the children to look at the pebbles in the container and see if they can spot any shapes or patterns in any particular one that resembles another: for example, an apple or an animal's head. Invite them to each choose a pebble that captures their imagination.

Talk to the children about how they can make their pebbles look more like their imaginary object by painting in some of the features, such as eyes, hair, petals and so on. Using poster paints, let the children paint directly onto the pebbles and then leave them to dry.

When dry, paint a layer of clear lacquer over the pebbles to protect the paint and create an attractive sheen.

Support and extension
Encourage younger children, who may find it difficult to visualise the pebbles as anything specific, to turn them into simple objects such as a football or a face. Older children might find it easier to use their imagination to create more detailed paintings, using some of the lines and ridges on the pebble as part of the pattern.

Further ideas
■ When you are out and about, look for any interesting stones and pebbles, and encourage the children to use their imagination with them.
■ Try using other natural objects, such as twigs and shells, for similar paintings.
■ Make a collection of painted pebbles – these make ideal gifts as paperweights or desk ornaments and are completely unique.

LEARNING OBJECTIVES
STEPPING STONE
Pretend that one object represents another, especially when objects have characteristics in common.

EARLY LEARNING GOAL
Use their imagination in art and design. (CD)

GROUP SIZE
Up to six children.

HOME LINKS
Invite the children to look around their gardens at home, or in the park, for unusually-shaped pebbles and stones that could be painted to represent something different. Show them how to dip smooth pebbles into a tub of paint to change their colour and create a collection of ornamental stones.

Magic painting

LEARNING OBJECTIVES
STEPPING STONE
Begin to represent some numbers using fingers, marks on paper or pictures.

EARLY LEARNING GOAL
Recognise numerals 1 to 9. (MD)

GROUP SIZE
Up to ten children.

What you need
A5 sheets of white paper; plain white wax candle; large tray; water paints (fairly bold colours); brushes; aprons.

Preparation
Use the wax candle to draw large, easily identifiable numbers from 1 to 9 (each on a separate sheet of paper). Ensure each child will have one of each number. On separate sheets use the candle to draw random shapes so that for each of the numbered sheets, every child will have three other sheets containing the random shapes.

What to do
This activity can be done in stages, starting with the numeral 1. Ensure each child has the corresponding numbered sheet and accompanying non-numbered sheets.

Organise the group so that the children have access to a tray of 'magic paint' and a brush. See who can find the number 1 first by brushing the magic paint across the papers. Work through the numbers in turn, and later on in the activity remind them to check their 'done' pile first when searching for a particular numeral.

Support and extension
Simplify number games for younger children by asking them to find the matching number. For example, show them a number 3, and ask them to match it with a hidden number, using their magic paint. Older children who are able to recognise numbers quite easily can play simple number games: ask 'How many wheels does a car have?' or 'How many eyes do you have?'. Provide the children with several hidden options that they have to uncover to find the correct answer.

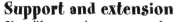

Further ideas
■ Use the candle to draw a number of circles, squares, or some other shapes and encourage the children to use their magic paint to reveal a specified number.
■ Instead of you doing the drawing, give the children the opportunity to use the candle themselves to draw a hidden number which the other children have to reveal and identify.

HOME LINKS
Ask the children to explore other materials at home that could be used to make hidden numbers that must be revealed using some other method. A bar of soap can be used in a similar way to the wax candle, and lemon juice will turn brown when it is dried in sunlight.

Bubble painting

What you need
Sheets of white paper; drinking straws; shallow trays or bowls; dilute water paint; scissors; aprons; newspaper.

Preparation
Make sure the trays are wide enough to allow the sheets of paper to be laid flat across the paint. Half fill them with the dilute water paint. Protect work surfaces and floors with newspaper and ask the children to put on their aprons.

What to do
Provide each child with a plastic drinking straw, and encourage them to blow air through their straws so they can feel it on their hands. Make sure they are competent at this, and know they must not suck their straws, before continuing the activity.

Encourage the children to blow into the paint trays to create lots of bubbles. When the paint has become quite frothy (preferably with a good mixture of large and small bubbles), ask the children to take a piece of paper and gently lay it on top of the bubble layer. Don't let it sink into the paint – you only want to take an imprint of the bubbles. Remove the paper and turn it over to see what pattern has been formed. Let the children take it in turns to make a range of patterns.

To make a more interesting bubble pattern, show the children how to take two sheets of paper, fold one in half then in half again, and use scissors to cut shapes around the edges of the folded paper. Open it up and there should be a symmetrical pattern of holes and shapes in the paper. Place this sheet on top of the other sheet, turn it over so that the patterned paper is facing down, and holding the two pieces together, dip the papers into the paint bubbles. Remove the top sheet of paper to reveal a pretty bubble pattern on the sheet underneath.

Allow the patterns to dry.

Support and extension
Supervise younger children to make sure they are not sucking instead of blowing the paint. Use smaller pieces of paper, perhaps cut into shapes to match the current theme. Once the bubble paintings have dried, talk about what patterns the children can see. Let older children make multiple imprints using different colours, such as yellow and blue paint, or red and green, for some really stunning results.

■■■■■■■■■■■■■■■■■■■■■■■■■■■■■■■■■■■■■■

Further ideas
■ Use the bubble prints as a background for themed collages and pictures. For example, a blue bubble picture could be turned into a sky collage. Cut pictures of aeroplanes, birds and clouds from magazines and glue them onto the bubble print.
■ Collect all the bubble prints, cut them into a variety of different-shaped circles and stick them on the wall to make a bubble frieze.

Autumn leaves

What you need
Sheets of white paper (A3 if possible); four trays (shallow, but wide enough for a child's flattened palm); red, orange, yellow and brown poster paint; cloths; towels; aprons; newspaper.

Preparation
Protect work surfaces and floors with newspaper and ask the children to put on their aprons. Have plenty of cloths and towels handy in case of spillages. On each sheet of paper draw the basic outline of a tree, or a few trees, with just the bare branches drawn in. Pour a different colour of poster paints into each of the trays.

What to do
Divide the group of children into pairs and assign a paint colour to each pair. Show them how to take it in turns to dip a flattened palm into their paint and make a handprint (with fingers closed) on the tree outline, which will resemble a leaf shape. They should try to include some leaves still on the tree as well as some that are falling. Encourage them to make different types of leaves with their hands – for example, by spreading their fingers, or by holding them tightly together, or even making a fist. Let them wash up and choose another paint to make different-coloured leaf prints.

Support and extension
Younger children may find it difficult to place their handprints accurately on the tree branches, so encourage them to create pictures of autumn leaves that have fallen to the ground. Older children can create a similar picture on a smaller scale using thumbprints instead of handprints, which requires a little more manual dexterity.

Further ideas
■ Collect real autumn leaves in as wide a range of colours as possible.
■ Talk about what else we see on trees during the autumn (conkers, acorns and so on).
■ Look for other objects that could be used to print autumn leaves, such as actual leaves themselves.

Creative colours

What you need
Sheets of card; tubs of paint in primary colours (red, blue and yellow); brushes; sheets of A4 paper; aprons; newspaper.

Preparation
Talk to the children about the principles of mixing colours. See if they know that two colours can be mixed together to make a completely new colour. Make coloured signs on the card with the name of each colour. Place these in front of the children to help them remember their colours.

What to do
Assign each child in the group a primary paint colour. Call out one of the colours (for example, 'red') and invite the child with the corresponding colour to paint a red circle onto their sheets of paper. Then call out a second colour (for example, 'blue') and ask that child to add their colour to the first colour.

When the children have tried all the variations of colour mixing, see if they can guess what colour will result, by asking them before they mix the paint. Encourage them to choose which of their playmates should be asked to add paint to their colour, and offer them guidance.

Support and extension
Younger children may need more repetition of the mixing of primary colours to reinforce the colour names and what happens when they are mixed. Paint a red circle next to a yellow circle, and then slightly overlap the two circles, mixing the colours to form orange. Provide paint in the secondary colours for older children and encourage them to experiment with various mixing patterns to see what colours result.

■ ■

Further ideas
■ Suggest that the children try an experiment to find out what happens when all the colours are mixed together.
■ Talk about shade: introduce white and black paints that the children can use to make 'lighter' or 'darker' versions of each colour.
■ Draw some simple shapes with easily associated secondary colours, such as an orange, a leaf and a bunch of grapes. Now ask the children which two primary colours are needed to provide the right colour for each shape.

LEARNING OBJECTIVES
STEPPING STONE
Show confidence in linking up with others for support and guidance.

EARLY LEARNING GOAL
Be confident to try new activities, initiate ideas and speak in a familiar group. (PSED)

GROUP SIZE
Up to three children.

HOME LINKS
Using the same principles of primary colour mixing, invite parents and carers to add drops of ink, paint or food colouring to a clear container of water to show their children how colours can be mixed in a different way.

Butterfly wings

What you need
The photocopiable sheet on page 67; brightly coloured water paints; brushes; aprons; newspapers.

Preparation
Make copies of the photocopiable sheet (one for each child). Cut out the outer shape to provide a butterfly template for each child. Protect work surfaces and floors with newspaper and ask the children to put on their aprons.

What to do
Give one butterfly sheet to each child. Explain that they are going to create beautiful patterns for their butterfly by adding small spots of paint in different colours, dotting it carefully all over the wings.

Encourage the children to choose a range of different colours and to make spots of paint in different sizes and in different positions on the wings. Show them how to fold the wings together and rub the paint through the folded paper in different directions, using circular or up and down motions. Open up the wings carefully and then leave to dry.

Suggest that the children try different techniques, such as flicking the paint onto the wings, or painting stripes to produce different results.

Support and extension
Younger children will need help in deciding how much paint to put on the open wings. Suggest they start by using only a small amount, opening the wings to look at the results, and then adding some more paint perhaps in a different colour. Talk to older children about symmetry, and how both of the butterfly wings look identical. They may want to make them even more elaborate by painting a pattern on one wing before folding it and making an imprint on the second wing.

Further ideas
■ Attach short lengths of cotton or string to each butterfly and hang them together in a corner of the room to make a butterfly garden.
■ Fold a piece of paper in half and against the middle line draw half a face. Help the children to paint in the features on just one half of the paper and then try to make a whole face.
■ Talk about why butterflies have patterned wings and how they use them to disguise themselves among the flowers and trees, as camouflage against any predators.

Tennis ball prints

What you need
Large sheets of paper of various colours; small tubs of dilute paint in primary colours (red, yellow, blue); tennis balls; aprons; newspaper.

Preparation
Ideally this activity should be done outdoors on a fine, dry day. If you are doing it indoors, clear a space in the middle of the floor and protect the flooring with plenty of newspaper. Ask the children to put on their aprons.

What to do
Let each child take it in turns to dip a tennis ball into the paint (without totally immersing it) and then drop it, paint-side down, onto a sheet of paper. The aim of this activity is to help the children develop control of where the ball lands and to try to produce a picture or pattern. To help them, you could mark a spot on the paper to give them a target to line their tennis ball up with.

Repeat the activity several times, using a fresh tennis ball dipped in a different colour of paint each time. Invite the children to try dropping the tennis balls onto the paper from different heights to investigate what effect this has on the prints. See how accurately they can drop different-coloured balls onto the same spot.

Support and extension
For younger children this activity is likely to produce more abstract pictures, but is very good for developing hand-eye co-ordination. Older children will find it easier to control the ball so that it lands quite close to where they want the print to go.

Further ideas
■ Pin the sheet of paper to a wall and let the children throw the painted ball at the paper. Try to make a line of prints.
■ Ask the children to see what happens when they dip and then roll the tennis ball across the paper.
■ Use the finished patterns as pretty and unusual wall hangings or to form the background to a sports collage.

LEARNING OBJECTIVES
STEPPING STONE
Persevere in repeating some actions/attempts when developing a new skill.

EARLY LEARNING GOAL
Show awareness of space, of themselves. (PD)

GROUP SIZE
Up to eight children.

HOME LINKS
Send the rhyme home, and ask parents and carers to help their children learn it.

Blow painting

What you need
Sheets of A3 paper; coloured water paints (made up so that they are fairly thick); drinking straws; newspapers; aprons.

Preparation
This can be a messy activity! Protect clothes, floors and working surfaces from possible spillages.

What to do
Provide each child with a plastic drinking straw. Encourage them to blow air through their straws so they can feel it on their hands. Make sure they are competent at this, and know they must not suck, before continuing.

Drop a large blob of paint onto a sheet of paper. Get the children to blow onto the paint blob through a drinking straw. They must hold the straw steady and control the strength of their blowing so that the paint travels in a straight line. (If they blow too hard it will splatter across the paper.) Then let them add extra blobs of paint, perhaps in different colours, and blow new lines in different directions.

Using a pencil, draw a simple racetrack, full of bends and curves, onto a sheet of paper and encourage the children to have a blow-painting race around it. See who can keep their paint inside the track.

Support and extension
Younger children will enjoy making a completely different pattern by blowing down directly onto the paint blob, creating lively splatter pictures in different colours. These could be turned into pictures of flowers or fireworks by drawing in the extra features. Draw the outline of a spider's web on a piece of paper and let older children try to blow paint in the inner threads of the web.

Further ideas
■ Have a paint-blowing race: encourage two or three children to start off at one edge of the paper and see who can blow their paint to the finishing line.
■ Draw some faces on sheets of paper and let the children blow paint to make some funny hairstyles.

Fruit and veg prints

What you need
Sheets of plain paper; trays of poster paint in a range of colours; a selection of fruit and vegetables (carrots, broccoli florets, potatoes, apples, oranges and so on); sharp knife (adult use); aprons; newspaper.

Preparation
Protect work surfaces and clothing. Halve the fruit and vegetables so that their shape is easily recognisable when it is printed onto paper.

What to do
Invite each child to select one of the pieces of fruit or vegetable and to choose the correct colour for printing them. Help them decide the colour of their fruit or vegetable, to name it and match it with the correct paint colour. Then, after dipping them in the paint, they can make a series of fruit and vegetable prints on the paper. Make sure they do not press down too hard to make the print so that some of the detail of the inside of the fruit will be visible in the print.

Encourage the children to print in patterns or in groups, and when the activity is complete display the prints and encourage the whole group to identify all the prints from their shapes and colours.

Support and extension
Help younger children to select their fruit or vegetable by asking them to make a print of their favourite (or least favourite) fruit or vegetable. With older children create a market stall of fruit and vegetable prints. Draw in the basic structure of the stall, complete with display area, and let the children stock up the stall using the prints.

Further ideas
■ Make prints of fruit on one sheet of paper and prints of vegetables on another. Do the children know which ones are fruit and which are vegetables?
■ On one sheet of paper draw a line representing the ground, and on another draw in a few trees and bushes. Let the children make prints of root vegetables growing underground and of fruit growing on the trees.
■ Use the photocopiable sheet on page 68 to make matching pairs of fruit and vegetable prints. Find the piece of fruit or vegetable that will create a similar result when halved and printed.

Stencil sounds

LEARNING OBJECTIVES
STEPPING STONE
Distinguish one sound from another.

EARLY LEARNING GOAL
Link sounds to letters, naming and sounding letters of the alphabet. (CLL)

GROUP SIZE
Up to ten children.

HOME LINKS
Once the children have grasped a few letters and can recognise them, encourage parents and carers to point them out on everyday objects, such as story books, outdoor advertising signs, food packaging and so on. Show parents and carers how to make letter stencils out of thick shiny card and let the children loose outdoors with a squeezy bottle full of water. See if they can make letter shapes on a path or driveway using the water.

What you need
Sheets of paper; pictures of everyday objects (a dog, a cat, a car, or an apple) from magazines; stencils of letters that correspond with the first letter of the pictures; glue; brushes; paints.

Preparation
Onto each sheet of paper glue one of the cut-out pictures, leaving room underneath for the stencilled letter to be added.

What to do
Invite each child to choose one of the pictures. Explain that they are going to find the letter that starts the word and add it to the picture. Ask the children to identify and sound out the first letter of their word.

If a child has chosen a picture of a cat they should sound out 'c' and then look for the appropriate stencil for that letter. When they have identified it, show them how to place the stencil beneath the cat picture and to lightly brush over it using one of the paints to reveal the shape of the letter that makes that sound.

Support and extension
Younger children will need help in making the connection between the letter sounds and the letter shape. Let them concentrate on two or three pictures that begin with the same letters to help them remember the letter shape. Older children will be able to name a larger number of letters, even those that have more than one sound, so choose a range of pictures to challenge them.

Further ideas
■ Display the stencilled letters and pictures on the wall as a home-made alphabet board.
■ Talk about the names of the paint colours available and what letters they begin with. Can the children choose a colour that starts with the same letter to paint over their stencils?
■ Cut out letter shapes for the children to paint over to create a reverse image of the letter.

Drawing

Help the children develop their dexterity and hand control using a range of materials such as pencils, crayons, wax crayons and chalk with these cross-curricular ideas for guided drawing activities. They will even use a computer mouse to create individual drawings!

Join the dots

What you need
The photocopiable sheets on pages 69 and 70; whiteboard/easel; pencils.

Preparation
Make one A3 copy of each photocopiable sheet and sufficient A4 copies of them for the children to use independently.

What to do
Before starting the activity, ask the children to count aloud from 1 to 9 several times as a group.

Take one of the enlarged photocopiable sheets and attach it to your whiteboard or an easel so all the children can see it. Invite the children to take it in turns to come up and connect the dots in the correct numerical sequence. They must each find the next number in the sequence and draw a straight line between that and the previous numbered dot, until the picture is complete. When all the numbers have been connected, ask the children what the finished picture is.

Complete the other A3 sheet in the same way and then hand out copies of the A4 sheets for the children to complete independently.

Support and extension
Prepare simpler pictures, numbered to 5 for younger children. Older children may be ready to complete pictures with numbers beyond 9 and could attempt to complete more elaborate pictures. Construct these so that finding the next number is more challenging.

Further ideas
■ Draw the dotted outline of a caterpillar or snake on long lengths of paper and fold into a concertina shape. The children have to join the dots, unfolding the sheet as they go.
■ Miss a number out of a sequence of dots in a picture outline and see if the children spot which one is missing.
■ Draw random dots on paper (or with chalk on a hard surface outdoors), but without numbers. See what pictures the children can create by joining the dots randomly, but counting each dot as they go.

LEARNING OBJECTIVES
STEPPING STONE
Say with confidence the number that is one more than a given number.

EARLY LEARNING GOAL
Find one more or one less than a number from 1 to 10. (MD)

GROUP SIZE
Up to ten children.

HOME LINKS
Suggest that parents and carers encourage their children to try dot-to-dot puzzles in activity books at home. Or they could use finger-paints to flick spots of paint onto a sheet of paper. After it has been allowed to dry, they should look for any obvious pictures that can be found among the pattern of paint spots by joining them up.

Real-life portraits

What you need
Lengths of wallpaper or rolls of computer paper; wax crayons or coloured chalks.

Preparation
Cut lengths of paper long enough for the children to lie down on.

What to do
Organise the children into pairs and explain that they are going to take turns to draw around each other. Ask the first child to lie down flat on the paper and the second child to choose a chalk or crayon and to carefully draw around their outline.

Once they have the basic outline, invite them to decide between them how to complete the picture. For example, ask them to think about what colour hair to add, what kind of clothes to draw in, and whether the face should be smiling or sad.

When the pictures are all complete, cut out all the 'bodies' and stick them on the wall at floor level to make a child-height frieze. Encourage the children from the other pairs to guess which body belongs to which child.

Support and extension
Younger children may find it easier to draw each other's outlines on a piece of paper already attached to the wall, with the second child standing flat against it. Older children will have fun adding extra features such as spectacles, moustaches or beards which could be cut from paper and glued on. Suggest they could turn their life-size figure into a character such as a post delivery person or a dancer by colouring in special outfits.

Further ideas
■ From the cut-out shapes work out who is the tallest and who is the smallest in the group.
■ Let the children draw around an adult and add accessories (such as spectacles or clothing in the correct colour) to show who they are.

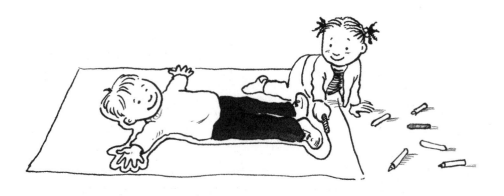

Finish the picture

What you need
Computers with a software program such as Paint installed.

Preparation
Load up the Paint program and use the mouse to partially draw some very simple images – for example, a ladybird without any spots, a house without any windows, and simple stick figures that have missing arms or legs.

What to do
Gather the children around the computer and encourage them to talk about what they can see on the screen, and then what they think is missing from the pictures.

Next, show the children how to use the mouse to draw in the missing parts of the pictures and then ask them to try it themselves. Let one child each complete one picture. Show them how to select different drawing colours and tools and how to use the 'fill' function to colour in the various parts of the completed pictures.

Demonstrate how to save the pictures so they can come back to them later. Provide opportunities for all the children to complete different pictures.

Support and extension
Select a thicker drawing tool and use very simple line drawings for younger children until they feel confident about using the mouse to control their on-screen drawing. Provide more detailed pictures to challenge older children who may already have experience of using a mouse as a drawing tool.

Further idea
■ Challenge the children to turn the partly-drawn pictures into something completely different. For example, the ladybird without any spots could be turned into a Daddy Longlegs with wings, or a spider with eight legs.

Mystery pictures

What you need
Clipboards; paper; pencils or crayons.

Preparation
Sit the children in a circle so that their focus of attention is on the adult in the middle who will be calling out the instructions. Attach sheets of paper to the clipboards.

What to do
Provide each child with a clipboard, paper and pencil. Ask the children to listen to a set of drawing instructions which they must follow in order to produce a drawing. This should be a simple shape such as a square, rectangle or triangle.

Give out the instructions for a simple line drawing using vertical, horizontal and diagonal directions. Give clear instructions to draw a line that goes up, left, down and so on and invite the children to follow these by drawing lines in the correct direction. Start with simple, regular shapes such as a square and progress to more complicated suggestions as the children become more adept.

Compare the children's finished drawings to see how alike they are!

Support and extension
With younger children spend time talking about the directional concepts such as 'up' 'down' 'left' and 'right'. Blindfold older children, by gently tying a scarf or tea towel around their heads, and see if they can follow verbal instructions to draw a picture using chalk on a blackboard.

Further ideas
■ Practise the use of directions by clearing a space on the floor and calling out directions that the children must follow by laying building bricks or pieces of coloured paper to complete a floor picture.
■ Make crazy wool pictures using a ball of coloured wool. Ask the first child in the group to hold one end of a ball of wool, and then the second child to take the ball of wool and follow verbal directions, such as 'straight ahead', 'left', 'right' until told to stop. Holding onto the wool, the next child takes the ball and follows another set of directions, and so on until each child has had a turn. What does the finished picture look like?

LEARNING OBJECTIVES
STEPPING STONE
Respond to simple instructions.

EARLY LEARNING GOAL
Sustain attentive listening, responding to what they have heard by relevant comments, questions or actions.
(CLL)

GROUP SIZE
Up to ten children.

HOME LINKS
At home the children can play blind drawing by placing a piece of paper on top of a book or other hard surface and then on top of their head so that they can't see what they are drawing. Parents and carers should describe a simple picture such as a car driving down the road or a boat on a lake, and ask the children to try to draw the picture!

Trace the outline

What you need
Sheets of tracing paper; soft crayons; sturdy sheets of clear plastic; felt-tipped pens.

Preparation
Draw some simple templates of stars, the moon, shooting stars and so on so that the shapes will be clearly visible through tracing paper.

What to do
Place the tracing paper over the pre-drawn picture templates and invite the children to trace over the lines as carefully as they can, first with their fingers and then with the crayons.

When they have had a few practice attempts, provide each child with a sheet of clear plastic and ask them to carefully trace the pictures again using bright coloured crayons.

When the pictures are complete, invite the children to use felt-tipped pens to colour them in and then stick them on the windows so that light can shine through to show the night sky during the day.

Support and extension
Younger children may find it quite difficult to trace straight lines of any length, so provide them with a ruler to guide their crayon along. Older children could work on several smaller images on one sheet to help them master the art of keeping the paper very still while they trace, and relocating to the correct position if it slips out of line.

Further ideas
■ Turn the clear pictures into magic lanterns by cutting circles in the sides of a small cardboard box and taping in the plastic, in the form of a window. Use a small torch placed inside the box to create the lamplight.
■ Try using different colours of transparent sheets and trace the outline of flowers, which can also be displayed on the window.

Blind drawing

What you need
Sheets of A4 paper; pencil or crayon for each child.

What to do
Ask the children to sit in pairs with their backs towards each other so that they can't see what their partner is drawing. Decide who is going to be the drawing leader and who the drawing follower.

The leader has to draw a picture, such as a house, a person or a car. Decide what this will be out of earshot of the follower. As the leader starts to draw their picture they must say out loud what they are doing, without saying what the whole picture is meant to be. For example, if they are drawing a house, they could say, 'I am drawing a square, with four smaller squares inside, and a rectangle that sits on the bottom line of the large square' and so on.

As they speak they are giving instructions to their partner, who must try to draw the same picture.

When the drawings are both complete, invite the children to compare them and to talk about the instructions that were given. Next, let the children swap roles and repeat the activity. Extend for another turn by asking the children if they can draw a scene, such as a group of fish swimming in the sea, the moon and stars in the sky, or a garden.

Support and extension
Younger children may need support in deciding which instructions they need to give in order for their partner to follow their actions. Encourage older children to give more detailed instructions, including terms such as 'next to', 'underneath', 'longer than', 'shorter than' and so on.

Further ideas
■ Try a similar activity using identical sets of coloured building blocks. The leader must construct a tower while instructing the follower how to build the same structure, describing the colour and position of each brick.
■ Give the leader a picture that has already been drawn, such as a picture of a kite. They must describe the picture to their partner in terms of structure, shape and the direction of the lines. Ask the children if it is easier or more difficult to describe when they are not drawing.

LEARNING OBJECTIVES
STEPPING STONE
Use talk to connect ideas, explain what is happening and anticipate what might happen next.

EARLY LEARNING GOAL
Use language to imagine and recreate role experiences. (CLL)

GROUP SIZE
Pairs of children.

HOME LINKS
Play a variation of 'Pin the tail on the donkey': on a sheet of paper ask a child to draw a face without a nose or a mouth. Let the child have a good look at the picture and then, blindfolded, see if they can draw in the missing features.

Pencil races

What you need
The photocopiable sheet on page 71; soft leaded pencils; crayons.

Preparation
Copy the photocopiable page to provide one sheet for each pair of children.

What to do
Hand out copies of the photocopiable sheet to pairs of children and look at the racing track together: point out the twists and turns, and the start and finish line.

Encourage the children to work in pairs and to practise flicking their pencils along the paper, using their wrist to flick vertically away from the body.

They only need to apply a light touch to achieve the result. The aim of the activity is to complete the racecourse by flicking pencil lines, without going out of the lines. The children must compete it in pairs, taking turns to flick. The first of the pairs to flick across the finishing line is the winner.

Ask the children to talk about how easy it was to complete the track: was it easier to flick with a long or short pencil? Or a fat or thin crayon?

Support and extension
Make a simple version of the racecourse with the track wide and fairly straight for younger children, and let them use crayons if they find handling pencils too difficult. Make a track that is narrower in some parts for older children so that they will have to control their flicking carefully or else their pencils will cross the line.

Further ideas
■ Have a Grand Prix or Grand National pencil race and have names for the 'cars' or the 'horses'.
■ Hold team races with groups of three or four children each taking turns to flick for their team. Use a different-coloured pencil for each child.
■ Use the same technique to create water pictures, such as fountains and waterfalls.

Wet chalk pictures

What you need
Different-coloured chalks; a shallow tray of water; sheets of coloured paper.

What to do
Show the children how to moisten the chalk by dipping it into a tray of water. Encourage them to use the wet chalk to draw pictures that produce a different texture to pencil or paint.

As well as drawing with the sticks of coloured chalk, encourage the children to use their fingers to rub in the wet chalk as they shade in the pictures. Warn them not to let the chalk become too wet or it will become very crumbly. Choose a theme for the activity, such as flowers or the seaside, and let the children come up with some lively pictures using this technique.

Support and extension
Provide different textures of paper (smooth, rough, shiny and so on) and encourage younger children to talk about what each type feels like when they draw on it with the wet chalk. Let older children create different colours by rubbing several colours of chalk onto the paper and blending them together.

Further ideas
■ Provide sheets of black paper and let the children create colourful wet chalk firework pictures.
■ Cut out circles of coloured paper and make place mats decorated with wet chalk patterns.
■ Imagine what animal footprints look like (find references in information books and look at the shape of paws, claws and hooves) and try to make some using the wet chalk.

Hang a basket

What you need
Blackboard/whiteboard; chalk/pens; paper; pencils.

Preparation
Imagine you are going to draw a basket hanging from the side of a house. Draw the wall, the hook and the empty basket on the blackboard/whiteboard.

What to do
This is a variation on the traditional word game 'Hangman'. In this game, the children must try to guess a three-letter word before the hanging basket has five flowers in it. A flower is added each time they guess a wrong letter.

Choose some three-letter words that include easily recognisable letter sounds, such as 'cat', 'hat', 'hut' and so on. Mark out a three-letter space on the board. Invite the children to think about what the word could realistically be rather than just making wild guesses at different letters.

Encourage the children to write the letters to form the words on their own paper as you write them on the board.

Support and extension
For younger children, who may be unsure of letters sounds, start off with the first and last letter already filled in and provide some extra clues if necessary. Use longer words (still with clear letter sounds) for older children who have a good grasp of letters and sounds. Make the words harder, or reduce the number of flowers that appear in the basket.

■ ■

Further ideas
■ Encourage the children to come up with alternative ideas instead of the hanging basket: for example, five currant buns on a plate.
■ Once you have found the hidden word, see how many more words the children can think of that rhyme with it.

Circles and squares

LEARNING OBJECTIVES
STEPPING STONE
Relate and make attachments to members of their group.

EARLY LEARNING GOAL
Work as part of a group or class, taking turns and sharing fairly, understanding there needs to be agreed values and codes of behaviour for groups of people, including adults and children, to work together harmoniously. (PSED)

GROUP SIZE
Pairs.

What you need
Paper; coloured pencils or crayons; square or circular objects to draw around; reference pictures of vehicles.

What to do
Ask the children to sit in pairs and explain that they are going to make a joint picture using circles and squares, using the objects available to draw around.

Invite the children to decide who will draw the circles and who will draw the squares. Taking turns, they must try to create a picture using just those shapes. Tell them that they can overlap the shapes, but they must take turns and decide between them where the next shape should go.

The children may choose to make a simple repeating pattern of squares and circles, a fixed image such as a car or a truck (complete with wheels) or a completely abstract picture. For example, if they decide to draw a train, they need to think about where the circles and where the squares will go. If necessary, provide reference pictures of buses or bicycles to get them started. Let the children explore your room or outdoors for more suitable objects, such as pebbles, bricks and coins.

Support and extension
With younger children keep the pictures very simple by introducing the idea of repeating patterns, which will make it easier to organise the sequence of turns. Give larger groups of older children a number of alternative shapes to draw around: they must still decide on sequences and what the end result will be between them.

Further ideas
■ Using a much larger sheet of paper, ask the children to work as a larger group to make a huge collage of many different shapes, sticking to the principle of taking turns to draw.
■ Let the pairs toss a coin – heads for squares, tails for circles – to decide which shape to use next.

HOME LINKS
Parents and carers could talk about the different objects around the house that children could draw around, asking the children what shape they think they would make. Items such as tinned food, empty shampoo and washing-up liquid containers and boxes of cereal could all be used.

Construction

Use these exciting ideas to explore and build with a range of materials – from paper bags, egg cartons, paper plates and boxes to socks, matches, pebbles, shells, drinking straws and Plasticine. The children will discover how to turn everyday items into creative masterpieces!

Paper trees

What you need
A selection of brown paper bags or brown parcel paper; green crêpe paper; glue; aprons; newspaper.

Preparation
Protect work surfaces with newspaper and ask the children to put on their aprons.

What to do
Explain to the children that they are going to use brown paper bags to create miniature trees, using a simple twisting technique.

First of all, show the children how to scrunch the paper to give it the appearance of weathered bark. Using a twisting motion on the paper they can form the main trunk of the tree. Next they can make branches either by tearing part way down the length of the paper bag and then twisting these strips into smaller branches, or by using a separate piece of brown paper and twisting it into the trunk.

Demonstrate how to tear the green crêpe paper into small thin strips and glue them onto the tops and sides of the branches to make leaves for the tree; leave to dry.

Encourage the children to make a set of trees that show the changes that take place during the seasons of the year. For example, add white or pink crêpe paper to make spring blossom, dark green paper for summer leaves, and red, orange, yellow and brown coloured leaves for the autumn. The winter trees can be left bare.

Support and extension
Younger children can use the twisted brown paper to make a sturdy central trunk and add the crêpe paper as leaves. Once they have grasped the technique of twisting more than one paper bag together, older children will be able to create some complex tree structures.

Further ideas
■ 'Plant' the trees in a shallow tub of sand or soil.
■ Talk to the children about Bonsai, the Japanese art of growing real-life tiny trees that are no bigger than the models they have just made.

Egg carton spiders

What you need
Pictures of spiders; empty egg cartons; lengths of pipe cleaner; scissors; paint; newspaper; aprons.

Preparation
Cut out the individual wells of the egg boxes, and cut the pipe cleaner into short lengths of around 6–8 cm. Protect work surfaces with newspaper and ask the children to put on their aprons.

What to do
Start this activity by having a look together at any pictures of spiders that you have available. Ask the children to look at the spider legs in the pictures and count together how many legs there are.

Invite the children to make their own spiders by pushing short lengths of pipe cleaner through the sides of the egg cartons. This will require a certain amount of dexterity to get the spider legs all the same length. To help with this, make marks on the spider 'leg' with white chalk and ask the children to push the pipe cleaner into the carton only up to the mark.

Remind the children how many legs their spider should have and where exactly these should be positioned on the egg carton body.

When complete, paint the spiders using bright colours and giving them stripes or spots on their bodies.

Support and extension
Help younger children by making small holes in the egg cartons into which they can guide the pieces of pipe cleaner. Older children could make an assortment of egg carton creepy crawlies, such as beetles or bumble bees, using paints or crayons to decorate the bodies and adding clear plastic for the wings. Talk to the children each time about how many legs they will need.

Further ideas
■ Make a giant woollen web in a corner of the room, attaching it to two walls with tape. Arrange the egg carton spiders on it to make a fun wall decoration.
■ Let the children make caterpillars and centipedes by joining several of the egg carton wells together and adding lots of legs.
■ When the weather is fine, organise a mini-bug hunt and look at some of the insects and spiders that can be found in the garden or the local park.

Paper masks

What you need
Paper plates; lengths of elastic or string; pencils; crayons; wool; felt and other decorative materials; sharp scissors (adult use only).

What to do
Give each child a plain white paper plate and explain that they are going to make them into a face mask. Talk about the different types of expression that a face can have: happy, sad, angry, surprised and so on. Suggest that the children can choose what kind of face their mask will have.

Let the children start by using the pencils or crayons to draw in the main features to provide the facial expressions: eyes, nose and mouth. They can then choose and add scrap materials, such as wool and small pieces of felt, for additional features such as hair, eyebrows, moustaches and beards.

An adult can use sharp scissors to cut out a small hole in the plates where the eyes are so that the children can see and small flaps in the noses allowing them to fold outwards when the children wear their masks.

Help the children finish their masks by attaching elastic, making small holes in the sides of the masks and using the scissors to push the elastic through. This can be knotted to hold it in place.

Support and extension
Encourage younger children to demonstrate the various expressions using their own facial features or by guessing the expressions on someone else's face. With careful supervision older children could use paper scissors to decorate the edges of their plates, by cutting a fringe or pattern or cutting out extra decorations to stick on their paper mask.

Further ideas
■ Sing some favourite songs and nursery rhymes about how we feel, such as 'If You're Happy and You Know It', 'Little Miss Muffet', and 'Humpty Dumpty'. See if the children can decide which paper mask best suits the words of each song.
■ Make a two-way paper mask with opposing features at opposite sides of the plate. For example, with carefully drawn features, a mask that appears to have a smiling face when worn one way, could become a sad face when turned upside down. Use the photocopiable sheet on page 72 and cut out the faces to make a two-way mask.

LEARNING OBJECTIVES
STEPPING STONE
Begin to use representation as a means of communication.

EARLY LEARNING GOAL
Express and communicate their ideas, thoughts and feelings by using a widening range of materials, suitable tools, imaginative and role play, movement, designing and making, and a variety of songs and musical instruments. (CD)

GROUP SIZE
Up to eight children.

HOME LINKS
Invite parents and carers to talk to their children at home about the things that might make them happy, sad or surprised and to discuss what other expressions our faces can show to tell other people what we are feeling.

Ten-minute motors

LEARNING OBJECTIVES

STEPPING STONE
Begin to accept the needs of others, with support.

EARLY LEARNING GOAL
Consider the consequences of their words and actions for themselves and others. (PSED)

GROUP SIZE
Teams of three children.

What you need
Small empty boxes (such as matchboxes, small cereal packets or similar); empty egg cartons; milk bottle tops; empty kitchen roll tube; glue; Sellotape.

Preparation
Cut the empty kitchen roll tube into shorter lengths. Clear chairs and furniture out of the way to provide an open floor space.

What to do
Arrange the children into groups of three and explain to them that each group must build a car out of the available boxes in ten minutes. Before starting the activity give them a few minutes to chat about their ideas for what they would like their cars to look like. Help them to consider the main features that they need to include.

'Ten minutes' is a difficult concept for young children to understand but they need to be aware that there is a time limit to the activity. Encourage them to listen to each other's suggestions. Because this is an abstract construction, they will need to be prepared to amend their designs and try different things. Invite them to use whatever boxes and materials are available and to use glue or Sellotape to assemble the various pieces. When the time is up, ask the groups to admire each other's creations.

Support and extension
With younger children, invite them to stick to basic shapes and ideas as it will take them longer to put their model together. Older children will benefit from guidance in terms of listening, planning and constructing the model. If they have difficulties assembling the pieces in one way, encourage them to try something different.

HOME LINKS
Ask parents and carers when they are out and about to look at the different types of cars and vehicles on the road with their children and to talk about what they might be used for.

Further ideas
■ Have a session to make themed cars – for example, try to design a car that could fly, or travel under water. What extra features would it need?
■ Ask the children to talk to the rest of the group about their models and what the various features can do.

Sock puppets

What you need
One old sock per child; glue; felt.

Preparation
Cut the felt into features such as eyes, ears, mouth, nose and tongue.

What to do
Invite the children to each choose an old sock and explain that they are going to use it to make a sock puppet character. Show them how to pull the sock on their hands and arm to make a puppet.

Show the children the felt pieces and explain that they can use these to make features such as eyes, ears, mouth, nose and tongue for their puppets. Suggest a suitable theme for the puppets, such as farm animals or people at work, and encourage the children to each think of a name for their puppets and a story to go with their character. The story could be about the different things that farm animals provide (for example, milk, eggs and cheese), or it could be about the forgetful postman who posts the wrong letters through the letterboxes.

Show the children how to attach the felt shapes, using glue, and encourage them to work their puppets to make them look as though they are talking. Leave the decorated socks to dry before using them as puppets.

Support and extension
Younger children will probably be happy to make the puppet first and then think of a character that suits the finished result. They will also need help in deciding where the features should go. Give older children a theme for their puppet-making (such as the circus or the zoo) and talk about the different kinds of people, creatures or characters they might find there.

Further ideas
■ Think of some favourite nursery rhymes or fairy stories and make some puppets that look like the main characters.
■ Let the children have a go at being ventriloquists – making their puppets talk, moving their mouths in time with the speech, but without moving their own mouths.

Matchstick maths

What you need
Used matches; sheets of coloured paper; glue; card; pen; aprons; newspaper.

Preparation
Protect work surfaces with newspaper and ask the children to put on their aprons. Using pieces of card, make a set of number cards from 1 to 10.

What to do
Start this activity by inviting the children to count to 10 together, holding up the relevant number card as they count.

Invite the children to use the matchsticks to make number shapes that they can then glue onto paper. The easiest way for them to do this is to add paste to the paper and then stick the matches onto it, rather than trying to add glue directly to the matches. Use the number cards to help the children decide where to start placing their matches, or draw in a pencil outline of the number for the children to follow.

Make the numbers quite large so that the children can achieve a rounder shape, otherwise the numbers can appear too square and will not be quite as easily recognisable.

LEARNING OBJECTIVES
STEPPING STONE
Use some number names and number language spontaneously.

EARLY LEARNING GOAL
Say and use number names in order in familiar contexts. (MD)

GROUP SIZE
Up to ten children.

HOME LINKS
Invite parents and carers to collect wooden ice-lolly sticks or paper straws and to help their children make number shapes at home. They could also spell out individual letters or simple three-letter words using the same technique.

Support and extension
Younger children should concentrate on making the numbers 1 to 5 until they are familiar with all the number shapes. For older children make up some simple mathematical puzzles, simple additions or number questions, such as: how many legs does a spider have? Ask the children to show you the answer using the matchsticks.

Further ideas
■ Use the same matchstick technique to create letter shapes.
■ Write a number on the paper and ask the children to glue the correct number of matches next to it.
■ Introduce the children to the idea of different types of number and counting systems. For example, use the same glued matchstick technique to make Roman numerals from 1 to 10 and see how they compare to modern number shapes.

Under the sea

What you need
Pictures of the ocean and sea bed; clean clear empty jars with lids (preferably plastic); sand; collection of small pebbles and seashells; jug of water; blue food colouring or ink.

Preparation
Before this activity talk to the children about the sea, looking at pictures of the ocean and the seabed and discussing the kind of objects or living creatures that might be found there.

What to do
Explain to the children that they are each going to create their own miniature underwater displays.

Give each child a jar and invite them to pour a handful of sand into it, moving it around in a circular motion to ensure that it is evenly spread across the foot of the container. Next, ask them to choose two or three pebbles and shells and to drop them gently on top of the sand. They can then hold the jug of water and gently pour it into the jar, trickling water down the side of the jar to fill it up to the top, trying not to disturb the sand too much.

Once the sand and pebbles have settled and the jar is full, let the children add a few drops of blue food colouring or ink to the water. Seal the jar with the lid. As well as decorations for the windowsill, the underwater jars can also be used as paperweights, to stop papers blowing around when the windows are open.

Support and extension
For younger children, provide shallow containers and use less water so that they can easily get their hands into them to place their shells and stones. Older children can create more detailed miniatures by adding items such as a sunken chest or a ship wreck made out of clay or Plasticine.

Further ideas
■ Cut out tiny slivers of silver or gold wrapper and drop them into the water to represent fish.
■ Use the same technique to make miniature jungles, dried riverbeds and deserts.

Our village

What you need

A2 sheet of paper; pens; glue; assortment of small boxes (matchboxes, cereal boxes and so on).

Preparation

Explain to the children that you are going to make a village. Ask them what kind they want to make: a large village or a small country village. Should it be in this country or abroad? Spread out the sheet of paper on the floor and draw in a few basic landscape features such as roads, parks, water and so on to create a base on which the children will create their village.

What to do

With the children, spread out the layout that you have drawn and encourage them to decide between them exactly which buildings are needed for the village, drawing on their own experiences.

Invite the children to use the small boxes and liberal amounts of glue to make features such as houses, schools, churches, shops, offices and so on.

Encourage the children to talk about what they are doing and why they are doing it as they work. For example, point out that some houses will be in rows along a road, while others might be close to the park; shops and office buildings should be close together in the centre.

Once the glue has dried, let the children paint their model village and surrounding landscape features to complete the scene.

Support and extension

Keep the village layout simple with younger children, and ask them to simply add houses in a design of their choice. Talk about which house they would like to live in, and why. Encourage older children to plan a more detailed village and add to it in stages over the course of a few days. They should talk to each other about what buildings need to be added and why and where they should be placed.

Further idea

■ Think about other countries and cultures. What would an African village look like? What kind of homes would it have? Use books and websites to find out about styles and designs of homes in other countries.

Straw mats

What you need
Paper drinking straws in different colours; Plasticine; aprons; colourful ribbons, or silver or golden yarn.

What to do
Invite each child to put on an apron. Explain that they are going to make mats from straws.

Let each child roll out a lump of Plasticine into a sausage shape (about 15cm long and 2cm in diameter) and place it on the work surface in front of them. Next they need to push a row of straws, not too close together (about ½cm apart) into the Plasticine. With the straws held firmly in the base, they should take another straw and weave it in and out of the vertical straws, from one side to the other, and then push the straw right down as close to the base as possible. Show them how to take a second straw and do the same thing again, only this time, weaving in the opposite 'in and out' direction to the first. Push this straw down to the base so that it rests on top of the first one.

The children should do this with as many straws as possible until they reach the top of the vertical straws, which can now be removed from the base. Encourage them to alternate the colour of their straws, or create a pattern within the woven straws by choosing different colours. They can create pretty straw mats by adding colourful ribbons, or silver or golden yarn in between the layers of woven straws.

Once all the mats are complete, display them in a chequered pattern on the wall.

Support and extension
The straws may need to be spaced a little further apart for younger children to be able to thread their horizontal straws through easily enough. Older children will have the dexterity to do this activity quite easily. Let them try weaving with different materials, such as real straw or pipe cleaners.

Further idea
■ You could use smaller straw weaving frames to make a set of drinking mats to make attractive gifts.

Traffic lights

What you need
Cereal packets or shoebox-sized cardboard boxes; black paint; red, green and orange paper; glue.

Preparation
Paint the boxes black and leave to dry. Cut circles from the coloured paper.

What to do
Talk to the children about traffic lights – what they look like, where they can be found, and what they do. Explain that the red light means cars must stop, the orange light is a warning that the red light is coming on, so cars must get ready to stop, and the green light means that traffic can go. Explain to them that they are going to make their own set of traffic lights.

Encourage the children to glue red, orange and green circles of coloured paper onto the box in the correct order that they appear on real traffic lights.

Use the traffic lights with floor road mats and toy cars.

Support and extension
Organise younger children into groups of three to make a set of human traffic lights. Each child must stick just one coloured circle (red, green or orange) onto a box, and then take it in turns to stand up and show their traffic light colour. Let older children make smaller models of traffic lights to place alongside the display of ten-minute motors (page 30).

Further ideas
■ Cut circles out of the sides of the traffic lights box and cover with clear coloured Cellophane in red, orange and green. Place a small torch or nightlight inside to make the traffic lights look even more realistic.

■ Demonstrate 'working' traffic lights by sticking a red and a green circle of paper on two adjacent sides of a box. Divide the children into two groups. Ask one group to stand against the wall at one end of the room and the other to stand against an adjoining wall. An adult should stand in the middle holding the box so that both groups of children can see their respective colour. Ask them to run back and forth from one wall to another while the other group is on 'stop'.

LEARNING OBJECTIVES
STEPPING STONE
Describe simple features of objects and events.

EARLY LEARNING GOAL
Find out about, and identify, some features of living things, objects and events they observe. (KUW)

GROUP SIZE
Up to eight children.

HOME LINKS
When they are out and about with their children, suggest that parents and carers look out for other kinds of lights that are used to control traffic, such as the flashing signs at pedestrian crossings and the flashing orange lights at school crossings.

10-MINUTE IDEAS: Creative fun

Collages

The ideas in this chapter show you how you can make interesting collages using a wide range of everyday items – including different papers, card and wool as well as natural materials such as shells, leaves, seeds and acorns.

Rainbow collage

What you need
Sheets of A3 white or black paper; coloured collage materials; glue; pictures of rainbows.

Preparation
Make sure the collage materials that you have available are in a range of textures and show all the colours of the rainbow: red, orange, yellow, green, blue, indigo and violet.

Include sheets of thin tissue or crêpe paper, heavy art paper and metallic foil papers.

What to do
Explain to the children that they are going to make a giant rainbow collage using the coloured materials provided. Before starting the activity, talk to them about when we see rainbows and help them to identify the colours of a rainbow in the correct order. Show them pictures of a rainbow so that they can sort the materials into the correct order of colours.

Help the children to paste a stripe of glue in an arched rainbow shape onto the paper. Starting with the colour red, demonstrate how to add papers and fabrics of varying shades of red to the glued strip. Let them continue with each colour in turn until the children have produced a rainbow. Aim to include lots of shade variations of each colour.

Support and extension
Younger children will need extra help organising the collage materials into colours, so provide books and website illustrations to help them. Let older children make their own smaller individual rainbow collages. They may also want to incorporate the rainbow colours into shapes other than the conventional arch.

Further ideas
■ Make a set of coloured paper hats for the children to wear and see if they can line up as a rainbow.
■ Think of some mnemonics that will help the children remember the order of the colours. For example: **r**ain **o**n **y**our **g**arden **b**rings **i**n **v**egetables.
■ On a showery day when the sun is shining, look out for a real rainbow in the sky and see how many colours the children can pick out.

Birdseed collage

What you need
Newspaper; A4 sheets of paper; glue; pastry brush; approximately 50 grams of birdseed/rice/lentils per child.

Preparation
Line the tables or work surfaces with newspaper to catch any fallen seeds and protect the surface from glue spillage. Try to keep all areas except for the paper free from glue to avoid 'unwanted' seed collages.

What to do
Explain to the children that they are going to make a collage using birdseed. Say that until the seeds have been added, they won't be able to see the shape of the picture, so encourage them to talk about what they want the final result to look like, and how they are going to achieve it.

Help the children to lay out sheets of paper and apply the glue with a pastry brush to draw their chosen shapes or outline; this could be a person, animal, house and so on. Invite them to talk about the shape they have made. Do they think the shape is large enough and clear enough? Ensure that they apply plenty of glue.

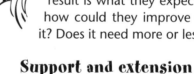

Invite the children to sprinkle the seeds, rice or lentils over the glue and leave this to settle for a minute or two. Then help them to carefully lift the paper vertically, allowing any excess seeds to fall off. Talk about what they can see.

Ask the children if the finished result is what they expected. If not, how could they improve or change it? Does it need more or less seeds?

Support and extension
Younger children may find the activity more interesting if they are producing recognisable shapes. Use stencils of farm animals or vehicles to help provide a clearer outline for the collage. Older children can work independently and can make collages using mixtures of the various seeds to produce a variety of textures.

Further ideas
■ Paste the glue in the shape of letters, numbers or simple words that the children will enjoy revealing, using the collage material.
■ Reverse the glued area of the paper so that the seeds and lentils surround the blank shape/letter/number in the middle.
■ Use dark green puy lentils and white rice to make more interesting, contrasting collage patterns.

Marvellous maps

What you need
Collage materials; coloured paper; pencils or crayons; wool; paper; glue; large sheet of card or paper; examples of maps.

What to do
Explain to the children that they are going to make a map, similar to those found in an atlas or on a globe. Show them some real maps of the countryside (or large cities) to give them an idea of perspective and the fact that they are looking down onto the features.

   Let the children decide what kind of map they would like to make – perhaps one that has lots of fields and farmland, or lakes and rivers. Provide a large sheet of card or paper and invite the children to choose pieces of coloured paper to represent features: for example, green for fields and parks, blue for lakes and ponds, grey for towns and cities. They can glue these pieces onto the base in their own design. Offer them lengths of blue wool to create winding rivers and streams, and brown wool to indicate the borders of fields and parks.

Support and extension
Show younger children pictures of real street maps to help them understand a bird's eye view and let them use the photocopiable sheet on page 73 as a template, inviting them to apply collage materials directly to it using a range of colours and textures. Older children can be more ambitious with their maps and make larger, more detailed map collages, perhaps showing whole countries or islands in the sea.

Further ideas
■ Ask the children to make a collage map of their bedroom or living room, as a bird might see it looking straight down.
■ What do whole countries look like from very high in the sky? Use books, atlases and website illustrations to give the children some examples.
■ What would a map of the desert or the North Pole look like? Are there any roads or rivers?

Alphabet collage

What you need
Magazine pictures of everyday objects; coloured paper; scissors; glue.

LEARNING OBJECTIVES
STEPPING STONE
Show interest in illustrations and print in the environment.

EARLY LEARNING GOAL
Know that print carries meaning and, in English, is read from left to right and top to bottom. (CLL)

GROUP SIZE
Up to six children.

Preparation
Cut out the pictures showing everyday items and paste them onto a sheet of paper. Aim to find pictures for as many letters of the alphabet as possible. Cut out letter shapes, in both upper case and lower case, to correspond with the first letter for each object.

What to do
Ask the children to look at the pictures that you have collected and to try and identify the letter that each word begins with. Invite them to find the corresponding first letter of the name of an object and to paste it next to the correct picture.

Encourage the children to find as many different letters and matching pictures as possible to complete the collage.

Repeat the activity with the upper case letters and a new set of pictures.

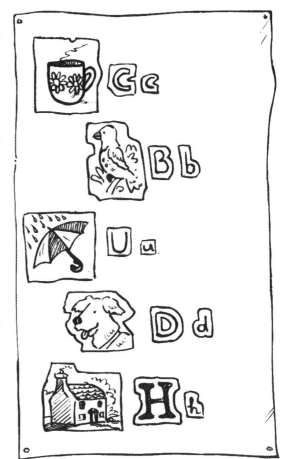

Support and extension
Younger children may find it easier to select a letter and paste that onto the sheet first and then to see how many objects they can find beginning with that letter to paste next to it. Include a wider choice of letters for older children and see if they can arrange them in alphabetical order on their collage.

Further ideas
■ Print the last two letters of three-letter words onto the sheet and ask the children to find a letter that could be the first letter of the word (for example, you provide _ **a t**, they can suggest **b** or **c** to complete the word).
■ Make cluttered collages out of cut-out letters and see how many letters the children can recognise.
■ Make word collages using different styles, sizes or colours of letters.

HOME LINKS
At home ask parents and carers to help the children look through old newspapers and magazines to find as many different styles of one letter as possible. Using plastic safety scissors they can cut these out and use them to make a collage of the letter 'a', or 'b', or perhaps to spell out their own initials.

Leafy bookmarks

What you need
An assortment of leaves; strips of cardboard approximately 20cm by 5cm; sticky-backed plastic; examples of bookmarks.

Preparation
Cut the plastic to a size that will allow it to be folded over the card bookmarks to seal in the leaves.

What to do
Show the children some examples of bookmarks and how they are useful for showing where we are up to in a book. Explain that the children are going to make one of their own.

Give each child a pre-cut cardboard strip and let them each select a few small attractive leaves to add to them. Encourage them to decide exactly how they want them arranged before using a small amount of glue to fix them into place. Finally, help them cover the bookmarks with sticky-backed plastic to seal them.

Encourage the children to select two or three small leaves from one type of tree or to use a mixture of leaves, depending on their personal preference, to provide individual bookmarks to take home and use. The finished bookmarks would also make lovely hand-made gifts.

Support and extension
For younger children, select a fairly large leaf and cut out the cardboard to match its shape exactly. They can glue the leaf straight onto the card and make a complete leaf bookmark. Older children might want to add further decorations to the bookmarks, such as colourful edgings or by drawing around the outline of the leaf with a glitter pen.

Further ideas
■ Cut the cardboard strips into unusual shapes (for example, to look like a tree). Add the leaves to the branches of the tree and colour the rest of the tree in brown.
■ Use pressed flowers or grasses instead of leaves.
■ See how many different types of leaves the children can name.

Funny faces

What you need
Faces cut out of newspapers and magazines; paper; glue.

Preparation
Try to find images showing as many different facial expressions as possible. Spread out the pictures evenly on the work surface to give the children a chance to see them all clearly.

What to do
Before starting the activity, talk to the children about our facial expressions and what they can mean. Practise making some together, starting with obvious ones such as 'happy' or 'sad' and progress to more subtle expressions such as 'scared' or 'guilty'! Emphasise that the children don't need to make any sound, just change their faces to communicate.

Next, invite the children to work together to make some face collages. Offer them the full range of facial pictures available and help them to select pictures showing faces with either similar expressions or contrasting expressions, such as

happy/sad, surprised/bored. Once they have selected the pictures they will need to apply quite liberal amounts of glue to the paper before adding the cut-out faces to make a group collage.

Talk about the faces you can see and ask other groups of children to comment on which expressions have been chosen.

Support and extension
Ask younger children to choose a cut-out face that shows a particular expression rather than letting them select randomly as too many expressions can be confusing. Encourage older children to link two faces together. For example, if they can find a face that looks happy they can add a face that is talking. Suggest that they imagine what the talking face might have said that made the laughing face laugh!

Further ideas
■ Use unwanted family or holiday photographs, cut out the faces and stick them onto the images of people or figures in magazine pictures.
■ Find faces with unusual expressions, where it is not clear what the person is thinking. Ask the children to imagine what the person might be thinking about.
■ Make a face out of faces: arrange the cut-out faces to form the features of one giant face.

LEARNING OBJECTIVES
STEPPING STONE
Initiate interactions with other people.

EARLY LEARNING GOAL
Respond to significant experiences, showing a range of feelings when appropriate. (PSED)

GROUP SIZE
Up to eight children.

HOME LINKS
Suggest that parents and carers help their children to make a face collage that tells a story. This can be a very simple made-up tale: on a sunny day a little girl goes out to play (smiling), then a dark cloud comes over and it starts to rain (surprised), the little girl has to go home and can't play with her friends any more (sad).

A sticky yarn

What you need
Pieces of wool (varying lengths and colour); sheets of paper; crayons; glue.

Preparation
Make templates on the sheets of paper by lightly drawing in patterns of wavy lines in pencil.

What to do
Invite the children to use the templates to make interesting and individual wool patterns.

Provide each child with a template and show them how to lightly brush some glue on to cover the paper. They can then select a piece of wool and press it onto the page following the shape of the pencil line. Once the first piece has been glued this will act as a guideline for the rest.

Allow the children to add further pieces of wool in different colours and lengths to make interesting patterns using a variety of shapes, such as spirals, corkscrews, squares or rows of wavy lines.

Support and extension
Keep the patterns simple for younger children and draw in a few simple shapes or outlines for them to glue the pieces of wool on to. Encourage older children to lay the pieces of wool close to each other. This requires a lot of dexterity and good hand-eye co-ordination, but it produces very attractive results.

Further ideas
■ Provide the children with copies of the photocopiable sheet on page 74 and invite the children to use the wool collage technique to add the stripes to the zebra.
■ Let the children colour in copies of the photocopiable sheet on page 75 and then ask them to add pieces of wool to help the monkey reach the bananas. Invite them to check how many bananas there are in each bunch and to add the correct number of pieces of string.
■ See what kind of pattern the children can make using just one very long piece of wool, adding several twists and turns to get it all onto one sheet of paper.

LEARNING OBJECTIVES
STEPPING STONE
Explore malleable materials by patting, stroking, poking, squeezing, pinching and twisting them.

EARLY LEARNING GOAL
Handle tools, objects, construction and malleable materials safely and with increasing control. (PD)

GROUP SIZE
Up to six children.

HOME LINKS
Suggest that parents and carers show their children how to try gluing lengths of wool in the shape of letters or numbers, helping younger children by drawing the outline for them beforehand.

Seaside collage

What you need
Modelling clay or yellow Plasticine; sheets of A4 paper; rolling pin; selection of seaside objects (shells, pebbles, seaweed, driftwood and so on).

Preparation
For each child roll a piece of clay or Plasticine onto a sheet of paper to a thickness of about 2mm to represent a bird's eye view of the beach.

What to do
Talk about any visits to the beach that the children may have made; remain sensitive to any who may not have been to one. Talk about the sand and the variety of natural things that get washed up on the beach such as shells, pebbles, seaweed and driftwood.

Give each child a sheet of paper containing the square of rolled-out clay and invite them to make a seaside collage using as many of the seaside materials as possible.

Encourage them to talk about the seaside and to imagine walking along a sandy beach when the tide has gone out. What kind of things might they see? Does the collage bring back happy memories of a day at the seaside?

Allow the children to choose from the available items and to carefully position them on top of the clay or Plasticine, pushing them down firmly when they are happy with their arrangement.

Support and extension
Younger children may find it difficult to remember a trip to the beach in detail. Look at picture books or seaside websites together to help them develop their imagination. Older children could try making objects they might find at the seaside from the collage materials – such as a collage crab or a boat using shells or small pieces of driftwood.

Further ideas
■ Preserve the seaside collages by placing the clay/Plasticine sheets in a shallow tray.
■ Encourage the children to imagine that their pieces of clay are the sandy floor at the bottom of the sea. Talk about the kind of things that might be buried down there.

LEARNING OBJECTIVES
STEPPING STONE
Try to capture experiences and responses with music, dance, paint and other materials or words.

EARLY LEARNING GOAL
Express and communicate ideas, thoughts and feelings by using a widening range of materials. (CD)

GROUP SIZE
Up to six children.

HOME LINKS
Ask parents and carers to help the children think of other ways of recreating other experiences using collages – for example, scrapbooks where they can keep postcards, newspaper pictures, photographs, or even pressed plants and flowers to help them remember special events and occasions.

Nature collage

What you need
A selection of leaves, twigs, seeds, acorns, sycamore pods, conker seed cases, grass, flowers; glue; sheets of card or paper; kitchen paper; heavy books or flower press; information books.

Preparation
Press the leaves and flowers with a flower press or between sheets of kitchen paper, weighed down by heavy books, and leave to dry.

What to do
Talk about a recent nature walk that the children have been on, either with your group or with their families. Look at the various nature materials you have gathered and discuss what they are and where they have come from. Explain, for example, that the seeds have come from trees.

Invite the children to use these materials to make a nature collage. Provide individual sheets of card or paper and encourage the children to each make a collage. This could either be an abstract collage or they could make a wild animal, such as a hedgehog or a fox, using the materials. Provide information books about British wildlife to help any children who require a reference.

Support and extension
Let younger children enjoy making an abstract collection of leaves and other items to make simple nature collages. Teach older children the names of some of the trees they might have seen on a walk, and their seeds. For example: horse chestnut trees and conkers; oak trees and acorns; sycamore trees and 'spinning Jennies'.

Further ideas
■ See what patterns the children can make using some of the materials. For example, held one way up, sycamore pods look like rabbit ears, held the other way they look like clown's feet.
■ Use small twigs to make a forest collage, gluing them onto the paper in the shape of trees. Glue some of the tree seeds to the bottom of the paper and talk about what happens to these seeds in real life.

Woolly sheep

What you need
Sheets of pink or black card; cotton wool; glue; large sheet of green card; felt-tipped pens.

Preparation
Cut out the coloured cards to give the shape of sheep.

What to do
Provide each child with a sheep template and ask them to give it a woolly coat by gluing and adding cotton wool balls.

Demonstrate how to apply the 'coat' evenly, which may involve breaking the cotton wool apart into smaller pieces, and remind the children to leave parts of its face and its feet free of wool. Add features such as eyes and mouth with felt-tipped pens. When the 'sheep' are dry, draw a simple farmland landscape together on a large sheet of green card and ask the children to glue their woolly sheep onto the hillside to make a group collage.

Support and extension
Younger children will find it easier to work with small pieces of cotton wool, or they can decorate smaller sheep using single balls of cotton wool. Develop the activity with older children, inviting them to add cotton wool clouds to a sunny day picture, or cotton wool moustaches and beards to a picture of a man's face.

Further ideas
■ Explain that some people count sheep when they find it hard to sleep at night. Invite the children to use cotton wool balls to make a picture of lots of sheep and give each one a number.
■ Sing nursery rhymes such as 'Mary had a little lamb' and 'Baa baa black sheep' together.

Paper crafts

Find out how to turn simple paper items such as bags and envelopes into puppets, use paper and card to make animal headbands and flowers, turn lengths of wallpaper into a hopscotch game grid and try some basic origami with these ideas.

Paper bag puppets

What you need
Paper bags (large enough to fit over a child's hand); paints or crayons.

What to do
Give each child a paper bag and explain to them that they are going to turn it into a nursery rhyme hand puppet. Talk about the songs or nursery rhymes they would like to sing and then help each child create a paper bag puppet that suits the song, such as Humpty Dumpty, or Little Bo Peep. Encourage them to think about whether their chosen nursery rhyme character is male or female, what they might look like and what their main features will be.

Provide paints or crayons for the children to draw in the main features for their character. When the puppets are complete, gather the children together and in turn let each child act out the relevant nursery rhyme with their hand puppet, while the rest of the group sing along.

Support and extension
Younger children may need help visualising the main features of their nursery rhyme character. Explain to them that they just need to include one or two main features, such as an egg-shaped head for Humpty Dumpty, or a spider on Miss Muffet's shoulder. Older children will be able to include more details, such as objects that their character might be holding.

Further ideas
■ Make stick puppets using paper bags decorated as faces or characters and then stuck to a ruler or wooden spoon. Let the children perform a puppet show by crouching down behind a table and using the sticks to move the puppets about.
■ Encourage two or more children to use their hand puppets to interact, like two characters from a nursery rhyme – such as Jack and Jill, or Little Bo Peep.
■ Make up a story about what hands do all day and use the paper bag puppets to act out the story. Include things such as: washing faces, cleaning teeth, putting on shoes and socks and so on.

Envelope art

LEARNING OBJECTIVES
STEPPING STONE
Use one object to represent another, even when the objects have few characteristics in common.

EARLY LEARNING GOAL
Use their imagination in art and design. (CD)

GROUP SIZE
Up to six children.

What you need
Paper envelopes with conventional flap seals; coloured pencils and crayons; Sellotape; scissors.

What to do
Explain that the children are going to use their imagination to turn blank envelopes into funny faces. Ask each child to choose an envelope and to turn it over so that the flap side is facing up. Tell them to imagine that the envelope is a face (either a person or an animal). See the illustrations below as a guide for how to incorporate the features into the shape of the envelope.

Invite the children to decorate their envelopes, drawing in features such as eyes, noses and mouths in the most appropriate places on the envelope flaps. For example, where the flap of the envelope comes to a point, this could be used to form the mouth, or the line of a person's eyebrows. Encourage the children to see what different features they can make out of the lines and folds of the envelopes.

Support and extension
You may need to demonstrate this activity to younger children to help them grasp the idea of visualising the envelope as a face. For older children provide cut-out paper shapes to represent features such as ears, eyes, teeth, hair and glasses from coloured paper for them to add more detail and texture to their envelope art.

Further ideas
■ Use the finished envelopes to send seasonal or birthday cards to friends and family.
■ On a fine day have a look at the clouds in the sky together and see if the children can see faces or objects hidden in the cloud patterns. Watch how the shapes change as the clouds move across the sky and encourage the children to describe what they can see. Find out if any of the other children can see the same thing.
■ Flick drops of paint onto a sheet of paper, fold it in half and spread the paint around the pages. Open them up and see if the children can make any pictures or shapes out of the paint images.

Rabbit ears

What you need
Sheets of white card; Sellotape; crayons and colouring pencils.

Preparation
For each child cut a pair of rabbit ears and a strip approximately 4cm in width, out of the card. Move chairs and tables out of the way to make room for the activity.

What to do
Talk to the children about physical exercise and how moving around helps to keep our bodies fit and healthy. Explain that this is the same for animals' bodies too. Say that they are going to pretend to be jumping rabbits, but first they need to make themselves a pair of rabbit ears.

First of all the children need to measure their heads in order to make a headband that will fit. Take one of the strips of card and wrap it around a child's head, securing it with Sellotape where it fits comfortably. Add extra tape to make sure it doesn't come undone. Repeat so that all the children have bands that fit.

Let the children colour in their rabbit's ears and then add them to their headbands, again securing them with Sellotape in an upright position.

Once everyone has their rabbit ears on, encourage them to move around like rabbits, hopping and jumping around the room.

Support and extension
Younger children will find it easier to jump with two feet rather than hop. Older children could try hopping on alternate feet and they could also try to twitch their noses like rabbits.

Further ideas
■ Make a collection of animal ears, including foxes, elephants, deer antlers, horses, and play 'Who am I?'. Choose one set of animal ears and one child to wear them. (They mustn't be able to see which ears they are wearing.) They should then try to guess what animal they are by asking the other children to act out the relevant animal movement.
■ Make tails to match the animal ears.

Wallpaper hopscotch

What you need
End of roll length of wallpaper; crayons; small beanbag or similar object.

Preparation
Unroll the wallpaper on its reverse side and mark out a conventional hopscotch grid with the numerals I to 9.

What to do
Line up the children and invite them to take turns to throw the beanbag onto one of the numbered squares on the grid. Invite them to say which number they have landed on.

They must then alternately hop and skip across the numbers in the correct order until they come to the square where the beanbag is lying. As they move, encourage the other children to say the number names in the correct order. When they reach the beanbag they must pick it up, return to the beginning and hand it to the next child. Encourage the children to count back down through the numbers as the child returns to the start.

Support and extension
Demonstrate the hop/jump sequence to younger children and let them practise it before they start the activity. Make it a little more challenging for older children by asking them to aim for the next number in the sequence 1 to 9.

Further ideas
■ Include some number puzzles by asking the children, for example, to throw the beanbag onto 'the square whose number is one more than 3'. Encourage them to say which square they are aiming for.

■ Make a hopscotch track with pictures of animals (or toy animals) in the squares instead of numbers. Tell the children that they must throw the beanbag and then move or behave like that animal (for example, a frog, a lion, or a duck) as they travel towards the beanbag.

Paper flowers

What you need
A real carnation; coloured crêpe paper; scissors; glue; lengths of pipe cleaner or florist wire.

Preparation
Cut the crêpe paper into circles (approximately 5cm in diameter), to provide three or four for each child.

What to do
Look at a real carnation with the children and encourage them to talk about its appearance. What colour are the petals? Does the flower have flat petals or crinkly ones? Introduce the names of the flower parts, such as 'petal' and 'stem'. Then invite the children to make their own carnations from paper.

First, they should scrunch the paper circles a little to give them a more realistic appearance and then glue several of them together in layers, one on top of the other. When the paper circles are dry they need to push one end of a piece of pipe cleaner or wire through the centre of the flower, folding it over at the end to secure it.

Assemble the finished flowers together to make an attractive and colourful floral display or place in a vase to decorate the home corner.

Support and extension
Younger children should be able to glue the paper together but may need help fixing the wire to the flower. Let older children use extra layers of crêpe paper to make their flowers look even more realistic.

Further ideas
■ Glue circles of white crêpe paper together to make falling snowflakes: stick them onto a sheet of black paper.
■ Make a night sky scene by cutting small circles out of aluminium foil and layering them in a similar way, to make twinkling stars. Arrange the stars in the shape of constellations. Look at picture books to give the children an idea of some of the constellation patterns that can be seen in the night sky.

LEARNING OBJECTIVES
STEPPING STONE
Manipulate materials to achieve a planned effect.

EARLY LEARNING GOAL
Handle tools, objects, construction and malleable materials safely and with increasing control. (PD)

GROUP SIZE
Up to six children.

HOME LINKS
Suggest that parents and carers provide their children with household tissue or kitchen paper to make paper flowers or similar paper models at home.

Colour dominoes

LEARNING OBJECTIVES
STEPPING STONE
Use words and/or gestures, including body language such as eye contact and facial expression, to communicate.

EARLY LEARNING GOAL
Say and use number names in order in familiar contexts. (CLL)

GROUP SIZE
Up to five children.

What you need
Card; crayons or coloured pencils in red, yellow, orange, green, blue and purple.

Preparation
From the card cut 30 small rectangles each approximately 5cm x 3cm. Draw a line on each card, dividing it roughly into two squares.

What to do
Give each child six cards and ask them to colour the two halves of each card in a different and easily distinguishable colour, but to try and use each colour the same number of times. Encourage the children to interact with each other in deciding which colours to use, in order to get a better spread of coloured squares.

Once this has been completed, the children can use their cards to play a game of colour dominoes. The idea of the game is to try and place all the cards in a matching sequence. Ask the first child to start by placing one of their cards face up on the table. The child on his or her left should then look at the colours of their own cards and try to match one with the first card placed on the table, lining up the colours so that they match. If they don't have a colour that matches, the next child in the circle takes a turn. As they play, encourage the children to wait and take turns. The winner is the first child to match all their cards.

Support and extension
Ask younger children to say the name of the colour they have put down to be matched against. Older children may want to make more elaborate domino cards by drawing patterns or numbers on them, but will need extra supervision to ensure that enough cards will match.

Further ideas
■ Use the cards to play Snap. If two colours are placed down together, the first child to spot this wins the cards that have already been placed down.
■ Encourage language skills by giving one child a coloured card, which they should keep hidden from the other children, who then have to guess the colours on the card by saying the names of objects that are the same colour. For example, they might ask: 'Is it the colour of snow?' or 'Is it the colour of grass?' and so on.
■ Use card copies of the photocopiable sheet on page 76 for the children to cut out the cards and play shape dominoes together.

HOME LINKS
Encourage parents and carers to play games with their children where verbal questioning and reasoning are required such as 'Twenty questions' where the child must guess the name of an object, such as a farm animal, or a type of transport, by asking questions.

Pencil rubbings

What you need
Paper; soft lead pencils; objects such as coins and combs from which to take rubbings.

What to do
Give each child a sheet of paper and let the children handle it. Discuss how it is quite thin and you can almost see through it. Place the sheets over some of the objects you have chosen and notice how you can see part of the object through the paper.

Tell the children that, using a pencil, they are going to make a rubbing of one of the items. Invite them to choose an object for their pencil rubbing such as a coin, a small ornamental brass or a comb – anything that has an uneven surface with varying surface textures.

By placing the paper over the object and holding it down with one hand, ask the children to use their pencils to lightly rub over the area of paper covering the object. A pattern should soon start to appear. Explain that some objects make better pencil rubbings than others because they have a more uneven surface.

Provide the children with a selection of rough and smooth objects and ask them to choose the ones they think will produce the best results. Prepare some pencil rubbings of objects in advance and see if the children can guess what they are.

When the children have finished their own rubbings ask them to share them with the group to see if the other children can make out what the object was.

Support and extension
Help younger children secure the paper and object they are working with; they must learn to use one hand to hold them steady so that the pattern will be even. Invite older children to do pencil rubbings against vertical surfaces such as tiled or plastered walls.

Further ideas
■ Try a similar rubbing technique on tree bark, brick walls, carved stone and doors to see how the different textures appear on paper.
■ Make a collection of paper coins from the pencil rubbings. Cut them out and stick them onto a sheet of card with labels showing the denomination of each coin. Display the finished work.

Paper chains

What you need
Coloured sticky paper; scissors; shallow tray of water; plastic cover for tables; aprons.

Preparation
Cut the squares of coloured paper into strips approximately 3cm wide. Put down protective covers for work surfaces and ask the children to roll up their sleeves and put on their aprons.

What to do
Divide the children into groups of four and explain that you are going to see which group can make the longest paper chain in ten minutes. Explain to them that in order to make the most of the time they have, they must take turns and work together in an organised fashion.

Demonstrate how to make the chains by wetting one edge of a strip of coloured paper and sticking it to the other to form a circle. The next strip of paper is then threaded through the circle and glued in the same way.

Invite the teams to start making their paper chains. Encourage them to work together as a group and warn them when half the time has elapsed. At the end of ten minutes, stop and gather the children together to measure all the chains and declare the winning team. Look carefully at the joins and see which team has made the most secure chains.

Support and extension
Younger children might find it easier to make the chains more quickly by using pre-cut pieces of Sellotape to secure the chains. Advise older children to encourage their team mates who are currently doing the sticking, and to plan ahead to decide who will make the next section of chain.

Further ideas
■ Encourage teamwork and communication by asking the children to make different patterns with the paper chains. For example, instead of making one single chain they could try to make a star shape by joining several chains coming off one central paper loop.
■ Make paper chain 'leis', or greeting garlands, like those used to welcome visitors to Hawaii.
■ Use the paper chains to decorate the room to mark festive occasions such as Chinese New Year, Hannukah, Divali, Christmas or Ramadan.

Ten-minute origami

What you need
The photocopiable sheet on page 77; A4 sheets of paper; pencils; ruler; string.

Preparation
Turn A4 sheets into squares by folding one corner across to the opposite edge of the paper and cutting off the surplus paper.

What to do
Introduce the children to the concept of origami and explain that it is an ancient paper-folding technique that comes from Japan. The word 'origami' means 'fold (oru) paper (kami)' in Japanese. Explain to them that they are going to make a paper butterfly without using scissors or Sellotape, using origami techniques.

Give each child a square sheet of paper and ask them to fold it in half, diagonally, to form a triangle. They should then fold this triangle in half to form another triangle. Then open up the fold just made and place the triangle on the table with the central fold pointing away so that it looks like a tent. Fold one corner across to the other side of the 'tent'. Open it up, and then do the same with the other corner, folding it over. Open it up.

The square sheet of paper should now be a butterfly shape. Invite the children to hang their butterflies up on lengths of string and suspend them from your ceiling or against a window.

Support and extension
Use the visual illustrations on the photocopiable sheet on page 77, as well as verbal instructions to help younger children follow the folding steps. They might also find it easier if the intended folds in the paper are marked out in pencil. Invite older children to use paints and collage materials to decorate their origami models and make them more original.

Further ideas
■ Look at photographs of butterflies for guidance on appropriate colours.
■ Use the photocopiable sheet on page 78 to make a mini frog Jack-in-a-box. Fold strips of paper measuring 8cm by 2cm in alternate directions, folding approximately 1cm of paper at a time, to create a concertina effect. Cut out the frog's face and glue this to the top of the concertina card, cut out the feet and glue this to the bottom to act as a base. Push the top circle (face) down and let go to see it spring up.

Paper pairs

What you need
Photocopiable sheet on page 79; paper; pencils; scissors.

Preparation
Make copies of the photocopiable sheet and cut out the pictures.

What to do
Invite the children to look at the pictures from the photocopiable sheet. Separate the pairs into two groups, and invite the children to each choose a picture from one group.

While the children are outside the room, arrange several books on the work surfaces and hide the remaining pictures underneath them, with one picture underneath one book. When the children return ask them to try to find a picture that will match the one they have, to make a pair, by lifting the books. The book should be replaced if the picture does not match. Once they have found a matching pair, they should line up, in order to show who found their matching pair first.

Support and extension
With younger children look carefully at the pairs before you start so that they are clear which pictures go together. Make further cards to play with older children so that they can find groups of objects: farm animals, vehicles, fruit and vegetables and so on.

■■■■■■■■■■■■■■■■■■■■■■■■■■■■■■■■■■■

Further ideas
■ Talk about different kinds of pairs – for example, opposites. Give the children an example of opposites, such as black and white, and then say a word and ask them to think what the opposite would be.
■ Turn the activity into a colour theme. Give each child a coloured piece of paper and see how many objects or pictures they can find in the room that match. How many objects can they think of that are outside the room?

Modelling

Make the most of a range of modelling materials – from Plasticine, clay, dough and papier mâché through to strips of aluminium foil – with these creative ideas that provide opportunities to practise skills and learn some new techniques.

Pass the person

What you need
Plasticine; table or plastic sheet; CD or cassettes and player.

Preparation
Use the Plasticine to make a selection of basic bodies (torsos) and body parts such as arms, legs and heads. Ensure there are enough parts for each child in the group to complete a body.

What to do
Ask the children to sit in a circle. Explain to them that they are going to play a similar game to 'Pass the parcel', but instead of removing sheets of wrapping paper when the music stops, they have to add various body parts to a Plasticine body. The child who adds the final part to make a complete body is the winner.

Place all the Plasticine pieces on the table (or a plastic sheet on the floor). Start the music and hand a Plasticine body to a child in the group, encouraging them to pass it to the child on their left. Stop the music and invite the child holding the body to select a body part, add it in the correct position on the body and then pass it on to the next child on their left when the music starts again.

Continue around the circle in this way until the figure is complete. Let the first child keep this model and start again by handing a body to another child. Continue until all the bodies and body parts have been used and each child has a finished model.

Support and extension
Try to make the bodies and body parts fairly large and chunky for younger children as they will find them easier to handle. Older children might enjoy adding finer detail, such as hands and feet, which will prolong the game and give everyone a chance to contribute.

Further idea
■ Play a variation to 'Pin the tail on the donkey', using a Plasticine donkey and tail. Blindfold and seat the children and place the tail-less donkey on the table in front of them. Ask the other children to give verbal instructions while they try to attach the tail in the correct place.

Moulded mugs

What you need
Sturdy plastic beakers or old mugs; modelling clay; rolling pins; boards; decorative items including beads and broken shells.

What to do
Invite the children to each choose a beaker or mug and then explain to them that they are going to completely change the way it looks and feels. Give each child a piece of modelling clay and ask them to flatten it out using their hands, or roll it out using a rolling pin (or another round object).

The children should then wrap the clay carefully around the outside of the mug, making sure the handle can poke through and that it does not fold inside the mug or underneath the bottom of it. Where the edges of the clay meet, ask them to press this together smoothly, ensuring that there are no gaps.

When they are satisfied that they have a smooth, even coverage of the mug, ask the children to choose some decorations, which they should then press into the clay. Let them decide how they want to decorate their mugs, either by leaving lots of clay visible (which they could paint over in a different colour), or by arranging the beads and shells in different patterns. Once the decorations have been added, the mugs should be left to dry.

LEARNING OBJECTIVES
STEPPING STONE
Begin to describe the texture of things.

EARLY LEARNING GOAL
Explore colour, texture, shape, form and space in two or three dimensions.

GROUP SIZE
Up to eight children.

Support and extension
Younger children will find it easier to use plain beakers that do not taper. Encourage older children to smooth off any rough edges and create a smooth even finish.

Further idea
■ Encourage the children to choose just one type of decoration and try to spell out the name of someone they would like to give the mug to as a present.

HOME LINKS
At home children could use any empty plastic container (for example, an empty drink bottle with the top cut off) to make useful items such as pencil holders and desk tidies.

Baked bugs

What you need
The photocopiable sheet on page 80; salt dough (see recipe below); beads; buttons; black pipe cleaner; boards; information books; access to a computer (optional).

Preparation
Use the recipe below to make up a batch of salt dough. Cut the pipe cleaner into short lengths, to make legs for the bugs. Make copies of the photocopiable sheet as a reference for the children.

> **Salt dough instructions**
> ■ Dissolve three cups of salt in approximately four cups of water.
> ■ Stir in about nine cups of flour, adding a cup at a time, to form a soft dough, enough for a group of five children.
> ■ Shape or cut the dough as required.
> ■ If left uncovered the dough will harden – or it can be baked at 200°F for 30 minutes or so.

What to do
Explain to the children that they are going to use the dough to make models of bugs, which will set hard once they have been baked. Talk to the children about the different kinds of bugs there are, using the photocopiable sheet as a reference. Find further colour references in information books or by looking on websites.

Give each child a block of dough on their boards and invite them to model their chosen bugs. Explain that they are going to make families of bugs so they need to think about how many bugs they will make, and their sizes. The bug bodies do not have to be accurate, but should resemble a hemisphere. Use the cut-off sections of pipe cleaner to add the correct number of legs.

Leave the models uncovered to harden, or bake according to the recipe.

Support and extension
Stick to easy and recognisable shapes for younger children, such as ladybirds. Let older children make several different kinds of bugs, while keeping the shapes and patterns the same for each family member.

Further ideas
■ Use information books and websites to look at lots of different kinds of insects, including bugs, bees, butterflies and so on, and compare the various body parts. For example, explain that they all have wings, but they are all very different kinds of wings.
■ Make a model of a ladybird or beetle with distinct markings or features. Ask the children to try and copy the model exactly.

Solar system

What you need
Plasticine or clay; large sheet of black paper; yellow paper; white card; diagram and/or model of the solar system (information books or website).

Preparation
Cut a circle of yellow paper and stick it in the middle of a sheet of black paper to represent the sun. Draw nine concentric circles radiating out from the sun to represent the nine orbits of the planets in our solar system.

What to do
Talk to the children about the solar system and tell them the names of the nine planets in it (Mercury, Venus, Earth, Mars, Jupiter, Saturn, Uranus, Neptune, Pluto). Give a very simple explanation of how the nine planets travel around the sun in a circle or orbit. Use pictures or website illustrations to help you.

Encourage the children to use the Plasticine or clay to make a model of the solar system. Show them how to roll pieces of clay into balls, remembering that the sizes of the planets are all different. Look at pictures of the planets to see which are the smallest and which are the largest. Show the children how to press the clay planets onto the sheet of black paper, one on each circle or orbit around the sun, until each planet is in place.

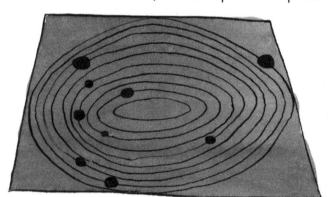

Encourage the children to move the planets into different positions around their orbit, but not to move them outside their orbit. Write out the names of the nine planets on pieces of paper and ask the children to help you stick them next to the corresponding Plasticine ball.

Support and extension
With younger children start off by learning about the orbit of the Earth around the sun, then talk to them about the other planets. Encourage them to repeat the names of the planets closest to Earth (Mars and Venus). Remove the planet name labels and see if older children can remember which order the planets should be in.

Further ideas
■ Think of other things that move in orbits (circles) such as the wheels of a car, a washing machine drum, windmills and so on.
■ Talk about the water cycle where rain falls on the ground, runs into rivers and into the sea, evaporates and turns into rain clouds and then falls again.
■ Find out about the life cycle of trees and flowers.

Pencil pottery

What you need
Newspaper; glue; various sizes of plastic containers, including cups and beakers; cling film; paint.

Preparation
Make up a large bowl of papier mâché by adding shredded newspaper to glue, to form a stiff consistency.

What to do
Ask each child to choose a plastic beaker or cup and cover it with a layer of cling film. Invite them to spread papier mâché all over the outside of the beaker (over the cling film) so that the beaker forms a mould or shape for the pencil pot. Make sure the cling film sticks out beyond the edge of the papier mâché for easy removal. Leave to dry. Carefully pull the beaker away from the papier mâché using the cling film. The pencil pot can be decorated by using paint or coloured sticky paper, and placed on the desk and filled with pencils and crayons.

Support and extension
Help younger children achieve a good even spread of papier mâché around the beaker. Older children may want to experiment with different shapes – for example, using the bottom half of unusually-shaped plastic bottles.

LEARNING OBJECTIVES
STEPPING STONE
Develop preferences for forms of expression.

EARLY LEARNING GOAL
Express and communicate their ideas, thoughts and feelings using a widening range of materials. (CD)

GROUP SIZE
Up to four children.

Further ideas
■ Use small pieces of chicken wire that can be bent or twisted into a shaped frame onto which papier mâché can be added.
■ Another way of modelling with papier mâché is to layer it on the inside of a plastic-lined container, such as a bowl or plant pot, and carefully lift it out when it is dry.

HOME LINKS
Encourage the children to use their desk tidy at home to keep loose pencils and crayons tidy.

Handprints forever

What you need
Modelling clay; aluminium sheets or trays; sheet of paper; rolling pin.

Preparation
For each child roll out a rectangle of clay onto a sheet or paper in the tray, approximately 5mm thick, and large enough for a child's pair of hands or feet (or both). Write initials or names on the back of each tray to identify them.

What to do
Provide a tray with clay for each child and invite them to make prints of their hands and/or feet in the clay. They can use their imagination to decide how to make the prints. For example, they could place their hands side by side, or one on top of the other, fingers open or fingers closed. They could place a left hand with a left foot or vice versa, or even make footprints that appear to be walking.

Encourage them to talk about what they are going to do before they start. Invite them to say how the clay feels and to talk about how hard they have to press into it to make their prints.

When all the prints are made, collect them together and see if anyone can recognise their own hand or footprints. Talk about the different prints the children have taken.

Support and extension
Help younger children make even prints by keeping their hands or feet flat and applying even pressure to the clay. Encourage older children to say whether they have made a left-hand print or a right-hand print.

Further ideas
■ Pretend the rolled-out clay is a muddy field and invite the children to use objects such as the tips of pencils or crayons to make sets of animal or bird footprints. How do these animals move? Is it by jumping with two feet together, or by putting one foot in front of the other?
■ Think of ways of using hands as an expression, such as waving goodbye, or saying 'Stop'. Encourage the children to practise these hand gestures and decide which ones could be made into clay prints.

Crafty nameplates

What you need
Permanent clay; small wooden skewers; paint; glue; glitter; scissors.

What to do
Break the clay into fairly small, easily manageable, pieces. Explain to the children that they are going to use it to model the letters of their own name and make a personalised nameplate for their bedroom door.

First of all, ask them to write down the letters of their name. This will act as a guideline to follow while they model the shapes of the letters. They need to roll out several pieces of clay into sausage shapes, around 4mm thick and 4cm long. Taking the first sausage, they need to bend the clay into a shape that looks like the first letter of their name, gently pressing the edges where they meet. For example, the letter 'b' needs one straight piece of clay, and one smaller piece bent into a semicircle and then joined together.

When the children have made clay models of all the letters in the name they have chosen, they can arrange them in the correct order on the table. Using a thin wooden skewer (no more than 1mm or so in thickness), they can then thread the letters together, with the entry and exit holes all on the same level. Cut off the sharp edges at each side with scissors. Leave this to dry.

Invite the children to decorate their nameplates using metallic felt-tipped pens, or by spreading a thin layer of glue across the top of the letters and sprinkling glitter over it, shaking off the excess and then leaving it to dry.

The nameplates can then be used to decorate doors, walls or furniture, secured with a couple of pieces of Blu-Tack.

Support and extension
An easier version for younger children would be to make just the first letter of their name, or their initials. Older children can make nameplates for friends and family, but may need help spelling out less familiar names.

Further idea
■ Use the same technique to make attractive place names that can be put on the table at meal times to show where everyone sits.

LEARNING OBJECTIVES

STEPPING STONE
Hear and say the initial sounds in words and know which letters represent some of the sounds.

EARLY LEARNING GOAL
Use their phonic knowledge to write simple regular words. (CLL)

GROUP SIZE
Up to four children.

HOME LINKS
Encourage parents to provide different types of materials, such as pipe cleaners and spent matches, for their children to form letter shapes and simple words.

Paper moon

What you need
Papier mâché; balloons; pin; black paint; string; newspaper; aprons; pictures of the moon in information books or from the Internet.

Preparation
Blow up the balloons. Spread out newspaper to protect work surfaces from wet papier mâché and paint, and ask the children to put on their aprons. Never leave children unattended with balloons.

What to do
Talk about the moon and the different ways it can appear in the night sky. Look at pictures of the moon in its various phases, such as 'full moon', 'half moon' and 'quarter moon'. Explain that it is not a flat disc, but in fact a ball or sphere, and that the bright parts of the moon are reflecting the sun's light, and the dark areas are actually shadow. The patterns of light and dark change as the moon moves around the Earth.

Give each child a blown-up balloon and encourage them to each cover their balloons with a layer of papier mâché. This needs to be fairly thick and evenly applied, and then left to dry. Ask the children to decide which phase

of the moon they want their model to demonstrate. For example, if they want to make a half moon, they need to paint half of the model white and the other half black; a full moon will be all white and a quarter moon will just have a thin crescent of white paint. Provide black paint for them to decorate their models accordingly.

Once the papier mâché is dry and rigid, use a pin to prick the knotted end of the balloon, allowing the air to escape slowly and gently. Hold up the finished models to show the light and dark areas to demonstrate that the moon displays its light and dark areas in the same way. Suspend the models with string and display them in order of their phase, starting with a left-hand crescent, a left-hand half moon, a full moon, and then a right-hand half moon and a right-hand crescent.

Support and extension
Help younger children apply papier mâché to their balloons successfully, without applying too much pressure and popping them. Older children might like to paint faces onto their models, similar to the face-like features on the real moon that create the so-called 'Man in the moon'.

Further idea
■ Sing nursery rhymes that include the word 'moon', such as 'Hey Diddle Diddle'.

Aluminium sculptures

What you need
Aluminium foil.

Preparation
Cut or tear the foil into a variety of shapes and sizes.

What to do
Give each child a few pieces of foil and invite them to experiment with the texture by twisting them into different shapes. Make sure they don't screw the foil up completely into a tight ball! Demonstrate how they can make long thin shapes, round shapes, or flat shapes.

When the children have modelled a number of different shapes, encourage them to try to join two or three of them together, again using a twisting motion. Using this twisting and binding together technique, they can make a whole range of models and figures, including people, birds, animals, trees and bridges. Put the finished models on display with appropriate captions.

Support and extension
Younger children may need help twisting the foil into a tight enough shape to make a model. Older children can use much larger sheets of foil and create life-size models of people.

Further ideas
■ Compare the texture of the original foil sheets with the texture of the twisted foil models. What would happen if the children tried to untwist the model? Would the foil return to its original texture?
■ Make lots of long thin twisted foil pieces and bend these into the shape of the letters of the children's names.

LEARNING OBJECTIVES
STEPPING STONE
Make three-dimensional structures.

EARLY LEARNING GOAL
Explore colour, texture, shape, form and space in two or three dimensions. (CD)

GROUP SIZE
Up to eight children.

HOME LINKS
At home parents and carers can help their children make miniature foil models by collecting pieces of coloured foil, including sweet wrappers and metallic gift wrap, and twisting it with aluminium foil.

Dough dice

What you need
Board game with dice; Plasticine or modelling clay; felt-tipped pen or paint stick.

What to do
Talk to the children about board games that require the use of a dice and show them one, rolling the dice to demonstrate. Encourage them to talk about why a dice is a sensible way to decide the number of moves that a player in the game can make.

Invite the children to make their own dice out of clay or Plasticine. Talk about the shape of the dice and look at examples of similar shapes (cubes). Ask them to try to make a cube shape out of the dough. The easiest way to do this is to form a rough cube shape and then flatten each face against the work surface, turning the cube over so that each face is flattened in turn.

Once the cube is made the children will need to add the correct number of spots, ranging from one to six. Look at the real dice and see how the numbers of spots are arranged. Point out to the children that each pair of opposing faces adds up to 7 (the face opposite the number six has one spot; the face opposite five spots has two spots and the face opposite the four spots has three spots).

Help the children to count the spots on opposing faces so that they can see for themselves. Using a felt-tipped pen or paint stick, in a colour that will show up on the clay, ask them to add the correct number of spots to complete their dice.

Support and extension
Younger children may find it difficult to grasp the concept of opposing faces adding up to 7, so let them add their spots in any order, as long as there is a different number on each face. Older children might want to draw numerals on the dice faces and these can be used to play simple board games such as Ludo or Snakes and Ladders.

Further ideas
■ Make a pair of dice and test the children's addition skills up to 12 by throwing the two dice and adding the score.
■ Paint different colours onto the faces of the dice instead of numbers, and decide that red = 1, yellow = 2, and so on, up to 6.

Beautiful butterfly

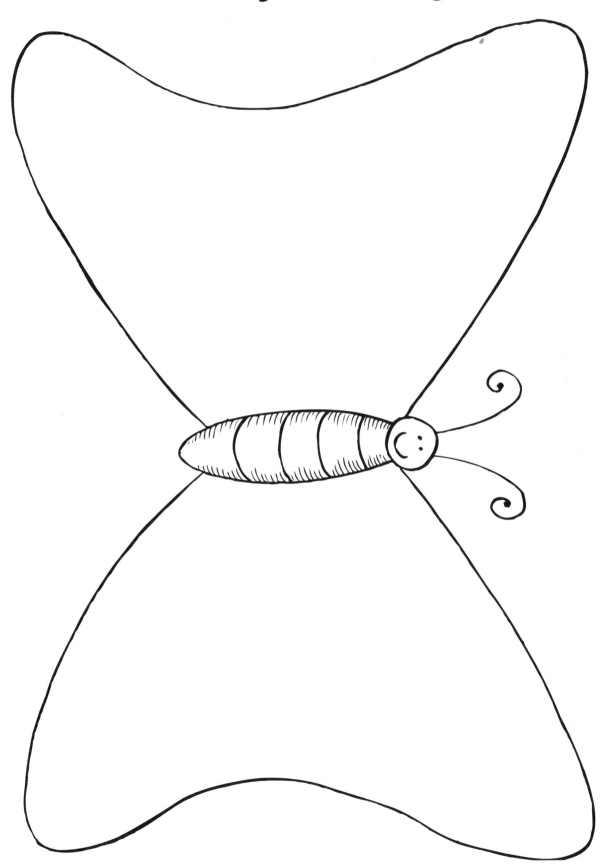

Let's print

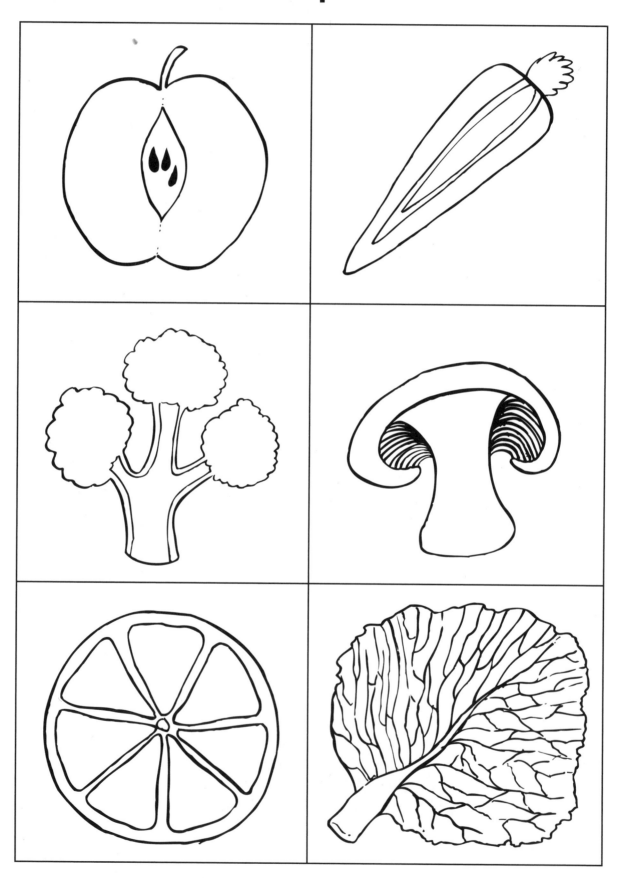

What can you see?

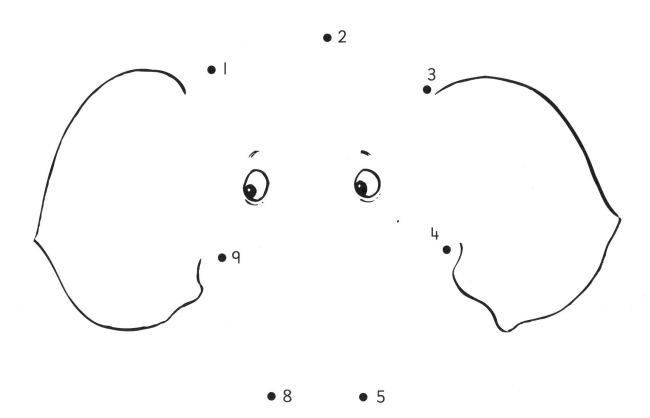

Make the picture

Join the dots to make a picture.

• 1
5 •

• 2

• 4

• 3
• 6

• 7

• 8

• 9

• 10

Take your marks!

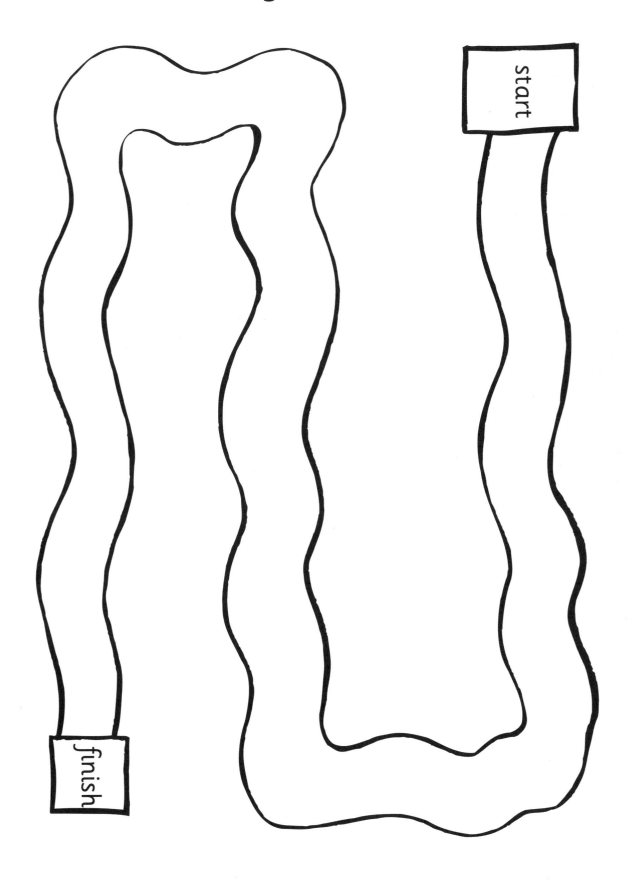

Happy or sad?

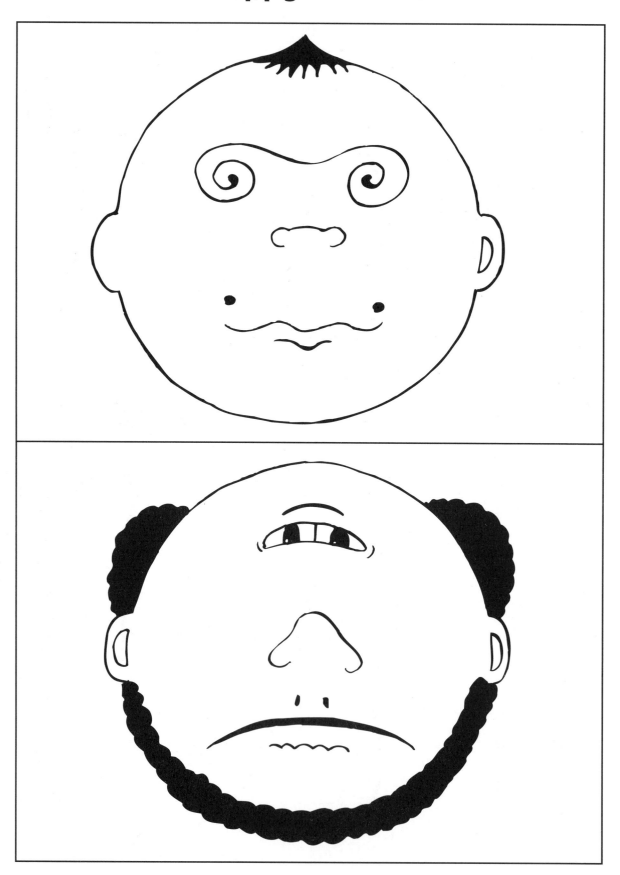

Make a map

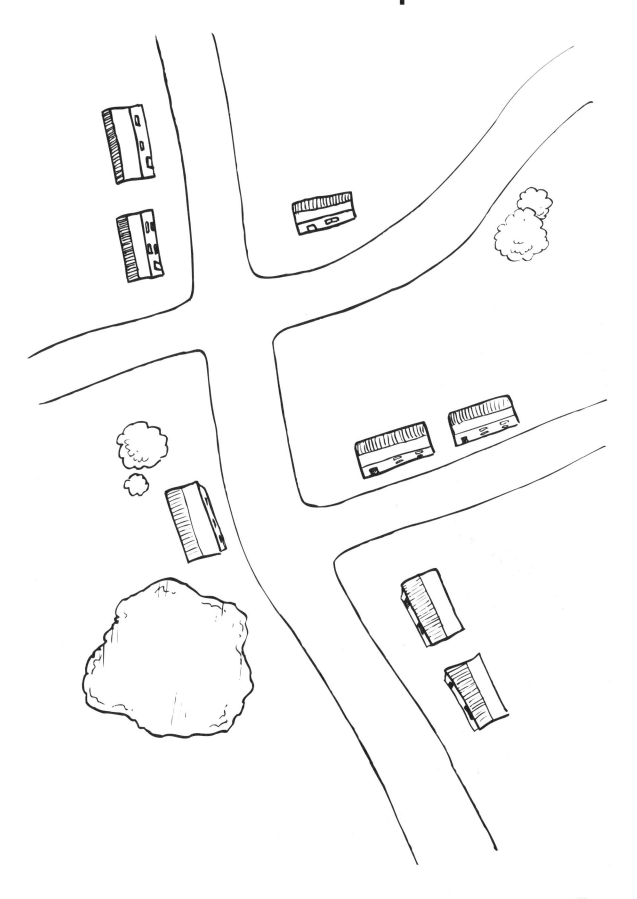

Zebra stripes

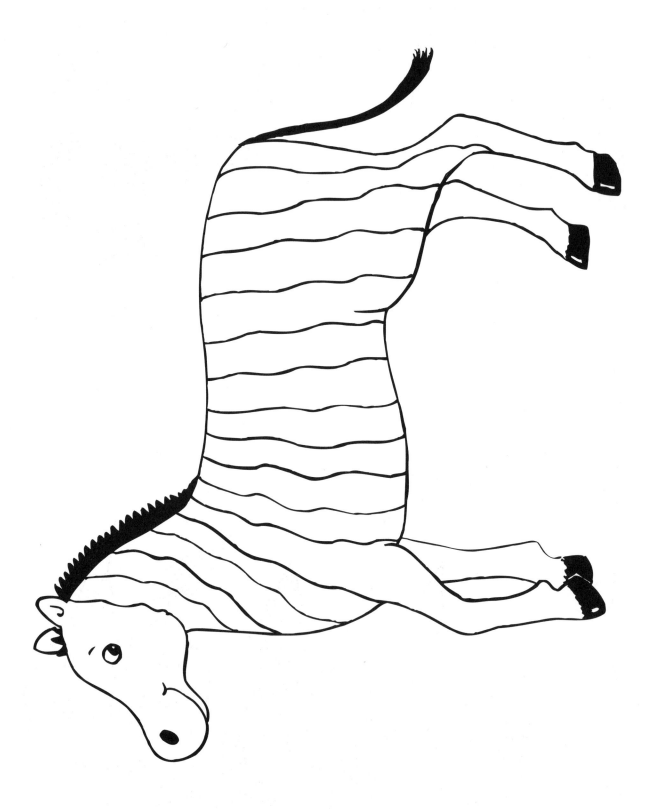

Hungry monkey

Can you help the monkey reach the bananas?
How many bananas can you see?

Match the shape

Make a butterfly

1. Make a square. Fold the corner of the paper over.

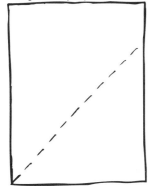

2. Cut off the small strip along the top.

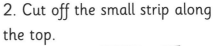

3. Fold the triangle in half.

4. Press the triangle down firmly.

5. Open up the fold. Place the triangle on the table, central point facing upwards.

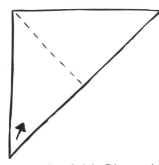

6. Fold one corner over. Open it up. Fold the other corner. Open it up.

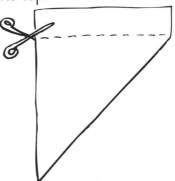

7. See your butterfly shape.

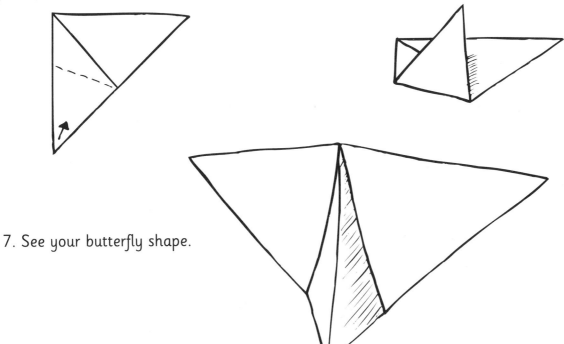

Jumping frog

Find the pairs

Make these creatures